The Darling Menopause

Deborah Crowe

About The Author

Deborah Crowe is an ex teacher and aid worker of 30 years, currently living in Dar es Salaam, Tanzania. Friends and family used to laugh at her descriptions of her fraught peri-menopausal days. She uses humour to create awareness of the need for women to take better care of themselves so that they can help save the planet.

DOGS IN DAR

A lady dog's insight into how her owner's deal with stress - or not - as the case may be. This will make you wonder if Eileen has a point. "Humans should learn from us, we don't need chocolate and tablets to get to sleep...".

This cartoon comic strip is set in Dar es Salaam, Tanzania, where the author lives. Deborah Crowe has written several stories based on her dogs' views on humans. Humans like herself who don't sleep enough, work too much and are too stressed. There will be more comic strips to come.

WWW.DEBORAHJCROWE.COM **TO GET DOGS IN DAR FREE THE DARLING MENOPAUSE - THE SHOCK**
A humourous diary about the discovery of the peri-menopausal world and life lessons from it.

"How long do you think it will last?" I asked. Thinking about two weeks with a course of antibiotics!?"Oh about ten years," he replied merrily. "No", I screamed. "No, No. No. I need to sleep sometime in the next ten years....I didn't really do that of course. I was too conditioned for that."

Come and find out what I DID do.

WWW.DEBORAHJCROWE.COM **TO GET THE DARLING MENOPAUSE - THE SHOCK**

REVIEWS

Wonderful writing, full of wry humour and a light-hearted look at life as we struggle to maintain our composure and keep a brave face during turbulent times. I thoroughly enjoyed reading it and could identify with the author's experiences. A great read to reassure yourself that you are not alone - cheered me up no end!

THE DARLING MENOPAUSE - SORTED

Diary part two - coming out the other end of the peri menopause - with yet more life lessons. It is not just the hormones

"I THINK THE HRT you have been taking COULD CAUSE YOU TO HAVE A STROKE AND SO YOU NEED TO COME OFF THEM NOW - TODAY - IMMEDIATELY..." I realised that had I had it ALL WRONG. It wasn't the hormones fault. it was the lifestyle for too many years - too much work. too much stress and not enough down time. My body just came and bit me on the bum to make me pay attention until I learnt how to redress the balance."

WWW.DEBORAHJCROWE.COM **TO GET THE DARLING MENOPAUSE - SORTED OUT IN MARCH 2017**

Preface

My autobiographical, humorous look at the world, **"The Darling Menopause"** ©, begins in in August 2014. Set in sunny Dar es Salaam, I chronicle my menopausal journey of the past 4 years to date, from my perspective and from that of my (now), 9 year-old daughter. I have gone from thinking I was suffering from Alzheimer's, to learning that "the change' lasts 10 years, and that there are 49 symptoms, in addition, to, the only one I knew about then, hot flushes. Everyone comes on trips with me to various doctors and hit and miss treatments, until I finally see a menopause specialist. But even then it is not all plain sailing. It is enough to lead a woman to swearing and outing herself.

I have found out that there is patchy, inconsistent information available. Mostly terrifying, especially if you are of a sensitive disposition like me.

Doctors are NOT trained in addressing the 50 or so symptoms that can come up and bite you on the bottom. Standard HRT is used, as if there are standard women. Even worse, lavender and hot milk are still recommended.

There are great Menopause Blogs around, mostly medical based. I want to complement these, with humour. In turn, I hope to raise awareness with a wider audience of women and men.

Someone asked me last week, "have you finished yet"? "No", I replied merrily, "I have 6 more years to go". **The Darling Menopause** © is here to stay.

I hope you enjoy it!

Contents

Hot Flush on Selander Bridge

My daughter has started a new school. This involves me in a drive to collect her. Mornings are fine as it is very early. Pick up at 2pm – a killer. At 35 degrees and in an old Toyota land cruiser with broken air con, I felt my hot flush starting in my toes and working its way slowly upwards. To add insult to injury, the windows are supposed to be kept shut in case someone grabs anything. "Bugger that", I thought. "They can have the bloody shopping and the car seats covered in dog hair".

There is always a traffic jam on the bridge – it is the only road in and out of the city. I didn't have my sweat rag on me, so I had to wipe my face on my top; the collar to be precise. I know that is gross but my hands were dirty. I got to school and phoned my husband, to let him know that I had done I my blog piece in my head. "I don't have a blog to put it into straight away". Pause, "ah yes", he says, "I said I would set it up for you". "Yes", I reply, "I have a HUGE need to rant about the menopause AND share it".

Coming back over the bridge – the drips of sweat collected under my chin. I need to do something about this soon or I will pass out on one of these afternoon pick up runs. It is not even the hot season yet either.

I am trying to get sympathy. Frankly some of it is my own fault. The heat isn't; but even the broken car is partly; I am unable to multi task anymore. I do try and get my husband to do everything with the car; he tries his best but with 2 old cars; it is a constant battle to have one working at any one time. I could have simply called the mechanic to collect the car and repair the air con. It sounds so easy, but if you read on, you will see how the simplest things TAKE ON a life of there own when you are peri-menopausal.

Back to why it is my fault? Well I stuffed up with the dosage of my HRT patch. I am on my THIRD type of HRT. THIRD. This one, which I recently got in July – is a drip feed of estrogen into my body to "smooth" out my moods. In other words to stop me being a complete cow, to anyone who was previously in my way at roughly 8am till 12 and from 5pm till 8pm. For the mornings I would call my husband and tell him whom I needed to murder at that particular time and he would suggest I went to the gym first. My poor child got it every night at 5pm. The guinea-pigologist who I finally saw in mid July – yes just two weeks ago – said, yes, children suffer when their mothers go through the menopause, AND that she would remember it. HRT is therefore not only for me, but also for her, hubs, the rest of the family and the world in general.

I am still digressing; it shows what a grasshopper mind I have. Anyway I didn't have enough Evorel 25s with me from the UK. The doctor had also prescribed 50s, as that was what I was supposed to progress to. I didn't know that though. I didn't tell anyone because it is not the first time I have done this and I don't know why I did/do it. I know the months of the year and the days in each month, but I seemingly can't count; as well as the usual long list of symptoms of menopause; that are kept a closely guarded secret until you think you have Alzheimer's, arthritis and heart failure all at the same time. The forgetfulness is terrible as is the feeling SO STUPID when it seems I can't do simple things any more.

I will never forget 4 years ago going to the doctor in Dar here and nervously telling him I had chest pains and swollen legs and thought to self; that I was going to die; I stayed awake all night to make sure I didn't die. How irrational is that? Staying awake wasn't hard, insomnia is part of IT.

The doctor looked at me in a new light and said suddenly, "How old are you"? When he realized I was 51 he muttered, "I think you need to see our guinea-pigologist" and ushered me out of his office as quickly as he could. I THINK I heard him say phew, but I can't promise. I duly made an appointment to see this retired specialist guinea-pigologist. Perfect I thought, I don't need to go and see someone in the UK, I have someone here where I live.

He explained to me that I was in the peri-menopausal period of my life. I had never heard of it. I asked how long it would last, genuinely thinking he would say a couple of weeks now that I had found him and he would give me a tablet for all my symptoms.

About 10 years he said. Imagine the following; I screamed and shouted and slid off my chair to the floor, yelling no, no, no it can't be. I need to get some sleep in the next 10 years. How come I didn't know about this, how come nobody told me.. Of course what I DID do was swallow hard and with a squeaky voice go, "ahh I see and why does it last so long"?

He explained in squiggly writing on a piece of paper I think I still have. I understood each sentence until it was replaced with another one.

By the end all I thought was holy fuck.

I was like a lamb to the slaughter, I had no idea that what he was about to give me, wouldn't work, that he wouldn't be available for follow up and that I was about to be in peri-menopausal hell for the next 4 years.

Back to today. Yes those patches. A lovely friend's husband is bringing the correct patches from the UK. As well as the other HRT tablet I take orally, twice a day. I don't in fact remember what the difference is between them. What I do know is, that if you change from 25s and 50s and your body rejects the 50s, as mine did – it is horrendous – with insomnia, pulsing of fingers and toes, bloating, constipation, exhaustion, gormlessness, inability to focus, waftiness; whatever you want to call it; probably shouldn't be drivingness – whatever that condition is. So I tore the 50 off and felt better, BUT the 8-10 and 5-8 yelling was back.

What to do? –

Oh yes reach for the anti anxiety tablets the OTHER doctor in Dar prescribed me. Standard procedure I now know for menopausal women.

It is 11am; I can now phone my chum without stalking her, to see if her hubs got back safe and sound. And more importantly does he have my drugs? Currently last oral in my possession for 3pm today and worse now patchless. Oh no! He doesn't arrive till late pm not early am.

I went to the gym. I love it so much, but I was so rubbish – I felt faint and dizzy and pathetic – didn't I say that is another part of the waftiness of suddenly depriving your body of a much needed hormone – in the right quantity – of course. I couldn't stop thinking of lying on the sofa.

Foolishly, after the gym I left for the shops. I hate shopping and never have the list, or enough money or sufficient brainpower to do it properly. I was after toilet paper; emergency situation; capers, anchovies, parmesan and nutella. I should have just got the loo paper and left. Unfortunately I stayed and tried to find the capers. The fuckers had moved from the shelf they had been on the last time I was in the same supermarket. I saw them and thought, "capers I need those". I had even said so to my daughter.

Capers Part Two

The remainder of the blog rant from the other day. I didn't realise I would get cut off mid flow as there was a word limit….

I then walked straight past them, as I couldn't be bothered to buy them that particular day. A BIG mistake. I heard myself asking a manager for help with where had the capers moved to. He didn't know, I asked could he find out, I had seen them before.

He smiled and didn't move. I asked again, saying that it surprised me that a manager didn't know where the stock was. He walked away saying he would come back, but he didn't, so I found him.

I never did get the bloody capers. They swore they didn't have them. I don't believe them. No one could possibly buy 30 or so bottles of bloody capers within 2 weeks in Dar es Salaam. NOT POSSIBLE unless the whole of the international community had planned a pasta putenesca extraordinaire.

Not good. It was only when I was home I realized I had had one of 10am episodes where I shouldn't be near others.

I also forgot the nutella.

Which is What and Dangerous Lifts

The problem, or one of them, with the menopause is that you don't know what are stress related symptoms and what are menopausal symptoms.

I suddenly felt panicky getting into a lift recently on holiday. I don't like lifts, I got stuck in 2 when I was young, and the image is still strong. I have also lived and worked in far too many developing countries with poor or no electricity supply to ever trust any lift anywhere. I have really getting phobic though and silly with it.

The problem in posh hotels is that there are only lifts on offer. The emergency stairs are hidden – not sure why. We stopped in Istanbul en route to UK in June. We stayed at the Hilton – posh, lovely food. Mirrored lifts – they help with the impression you are in a room not a lift. I did still go to the loo each time before; I got in the lift in case we got stuck. Those are the sorts of lifts that you are supposed to never get stuck in.

Bugger me of course we did.

For about a nano second, but that is enough for a chest pang. We were on the 24th floor and it stayed on the 16th and wouldn't let us out. I called the help button and said we were stuck. The door opened and they said they would send an engineer. Meanwhile as I was with my daughter, I was pretending it was fine and that these things happen. She wasn't fazed, but neither of us really wanted to spend the day on the 16th floor lobby. I had to call twice more before the engineer came. He took us to the 24th floor and told us that we had to use our room card when we got in the lift and then press our floor button.

I was indignant – why hadn't they told us at reception when we'd checked in?

I then read on the website of a well woman clinic; the one where I finally saw the in July 2014 gynaecologist doctor; and it listed heightened agoraphobia and claustrophobia are also symptoms of menopause. I thought I had bottomed out on the list of symptoms and was becoming seasoned. But NO.

Back to today. I just gave my husband a lift to his office. Remember the 2-car family, with one car operational at any one time. I overshot the turning to his office. I rarely get anywhere without doing that. He is not usually in the car though, I have to say. It is more often children; who thankfully are often not aware of where they are or where they are going. Such is their faith in the grown up driving them. Poor darlings. They don't know the risks they run with peri-menopausal women.

I tend to have to suddenly swerve into lots of dirt roads to turn round. Never an elegant 3-point turn, a hot sweaty 7-point turn with no power assisted steering is my norm.

Birdbrain could be both stress and menopause. Or stress of the menopause? Who can tell?

I did watch the birds this morning. Having stopped working 18 hours a day, since I closed my business in June, has certainly made that possible. Maybe I should stop wondering when and how stress merges into the menopause and vice versa. I need to stop over-thinking – and become shallower. I will see how I do for the rest of the day.

Shallow and Grumpy

Despite a week's gap, I remember leaving the last post with the desire to be shallower. Did I make it? Well, last week despite the supposedly correct patch, correct tablets, AND many of them; I was rather YELLY in the afternoons. My daughter was very helpful and asked me if I had had my afternoon tablet each day. It was roughly between 3pm – 5pm, so something clearly wasn't working. By Thursday, she told me she didn't think she could take me being this ghastly.

Mornings were great she fedback. Considering the potential for yelliness in the mornings; she is right; they are going swimmingly. Last Monday morning at school, I had seen a sign attached to the classroom window. The basic message was be nice to your children, don't yell, love them and give them surprises. I felt guilty reading it, and left school vowing to not yell and to get her a surprise present.

But the week turned out otherwise or rather the afternoons did. I am working on those – shallow or otherwise.

Hair Loss IS Sexy

Of course it isn't, but I thought that might catch your eye. I went to the gym today and did 90 minutes of Yoga. Fabulous, absolutely fabulous. My yin and yang were doing what they were supposed to do; I was breathing properly without feeling faint; all marvellous. When I got back home we still had power. Unusual for this time of year and we have no generator. I turned on the hot water switch and decided to splash out (pardon the pun) on a full body shower and hair wash.

I know that makes me sound rather unclean. I am not, I promise but when there is no power, there is no water, as the power is needed for the water pump. I hear connections going off in people's heads and them thinking ahh…. I see. No problem to have a cold wash using the water from the bucket in the bathroom kept especially for those occasions. However, I have to confess, despite my hardiness for washing with a jug and living without hot water; this doesn't extend to washing my hair in cold water. In my view, people wash their hair far too much. Once or twice a week is plenty even for sweaty children and models.

I am so lucky, I also have another reason. I know, I know, you have been waiting for that Menopause Moment – an MM.

Yes, hair loss is another of those darling little symptoms. So you can understand now, my own very good reason, NOT to be rushing for the shampoo each day.

Mind you, I have never checked with the doctor. Does all the hair WAIT until you wash it; and then come out in a larger clump in the weekly wash, just to spite you?
Oh well as I am shallow, I will leave that train of thought well alone.

My shower today with hot water was lovely, and so is my hair.

See The Good At 4am

Yes well, I have been trying to see the good. But

sometimes I just forget, often for several days.

This morning, I was awake at 4am and trying to find the good in that. It was hard, as frankly, I was pissed off. It seems wrong, to start the day feeling cross about being awake when you don't want to be. I lay there thinking about seeing the good and really was challenged to find any. Then it came to me. I realised that if I got up and went into the living room mosquitoes wouldn't bite me. It is the cool season and the house is wonderfully free of mossies at the moment. I think that is a good attempt at seeing the good at 4am. Shallow but not bad.

As I've mentioned before; difficulty falling asleep, waking up frequently during the night, difficulty returning to sleep and waking up too early in the morning; these are all part of the FUN of the peri-menopausal DECADE before you reach fully fledged menopausal – dom. I googled, "why does menopause give you insomnia" and a long, JOLLY list of articles and books is wonderful.

Full of titles such as; The Change Before the Change: Everything You Need to Know to Stay Healthy in the Decade Before Menopause by Laura E. Corio, Linda G. Kahn· BANTAM DELL· Paperback· 448 pages· ISBN 0553380311

Could It Be Perimenopause?: How Women 35-50 Can Overcome Forgetfulness, Mood Swings, Insomnia, Weight Gain, Sexual Dysfunction, and Other Telltale

Signs of Hormonal Imbalance. by Steven R. Goldstein, Laurie Ashner · Vermilion · Paperback · 242 pages · ISBN 0091816696

I have read neither, I am sure they are brilliant. BUT don't the titles make you want to run from them screaming? I still can't get over the fact that I DIDN'T KNOW peri-menopause was coming to get me – and thousands of others.

How come I didn't know?

I feel sure that a hint, an idea, a warning, a clue should have been given to me by someone, a doctor perhaps? I should have seen something, a glossy pamphlet or brochure?

You don't need to read anything, except THIS blog; because I will tell you, why you can't sleep for 10 years. Your flipping ovaries decrease the production of progesterone – which is a sleep-promoting hormone.

I know in time that, I have to come to terms with my lot; but not yet; no bloody way. I am still outraged. How come I knew so little about these wonderful hormones? I never appreciated them when I had enough of them, as I thought they were mine to keep.

Enough to snore sweetly through the whole night.

THE WHOLE NIGHT.

EVERY NIGHT.

Be At One With Nature

My yoga teacher, who I admire greatly, used that phrase yesterday.

We both had sore bums, from holding our poses for so long the day before. She asked me, if I had felt different emotionally after the class. I said I didn't know because I was on HRT and so couldn't tell what was me and what was medication. She replied that, humans fight nature every step of the way, and that menopause was part of a natural cycle of life and that I shouldn't take tablets. I don't doubt her at all; my dilemma though is that the phrase "be at one with nature" evokes positive not negative thoughts. How come then that the screaming habdabs because of lack of sleep are also part of that lovely, darling natural cycle of menopausal life as well?

But those very habdabs aren't very nice for my family or me or anyone left still talking to me. Bring on the drugs I say, unfortunately, I am not convinced they work for me completely either. Maybe I am just one in a million. Or another way to look at it is, I am totally snookered.

We didn't have much time to talk more and she has now

left on a trip. I will ask her when she gets back, what you are supposed to do instead of the tablets to "smooth" out those darling little mood swings.

Oh yes, and how to get some bloody sleep for longer than 20 minutes at a time; and just to be really greedy; in bed and at night time, rather than on the sofa, in the car, on a chair or just about anywhere else.

The problem is that, IF she mentions lavender oil, hot milk and lots of "me" time, I just might freak out. I don't WANT lots of me time and massages; I just want to be able to finish a fricking sentence without gazing into middle earth. Or have someone ask me gently if I am all right. I want to walk down the corridor and know why I am bloody doing it. And I want to NOT yell at my loved ones.

Is the peri-menopause "new"? Is it because women are living longer? Was it better when we all died off young – a rather drastic way to avoid it I admit? I will wait and see what the teacher says and then share.

Many Paws

I do hope you all get it. It is so great.

My daughter asked me again about the "many paws" last night. She is only 9, and does so well to remember the list of symptoms and that none of it is her fault, blah, blah blah. For her, of course it is really simple, the nice mum and the evil one. She then noticed that it sounded like "manypaws" and laughed her head off. We have three dogs you see.

I read my blog posts out loud to her last night. Not your average bedtime story I would say, but she asked. I warned her that I had used some rude words. She was riveted and I have to say she loved all of them and thought that I was very clever. The very nice mum finished putting her to bed. Actually I was asleep before her. Squeezed into her single bed, I was vaguely aware of some sort of noise in my ear. It was her talking, but I simply couldn't answer. I woke up at 3am,with my leg half out of the wooden frame; and with what felt like wooden slat marks etched into my body; where, I had squashed the foam mattress down into the bedframe with my weight.

It took what felt like an hour to move her off me, collect my bits of body, disengage myself from parts of the mosquito net, and get up. Mindful of seeing the good and all that stuff, I decided that I was going to meditate and have deep thoughts.

BUT, I am afraid I saw my husband's computer just looking at me. Before I knew it, Episode 1, Season 4 of Game of Thrones was on, fantastic. I settled into the comfiest part of the sofa.

Not for long sadly.

Busted. My husband was up and wandering around and told me to get back to bed my own this time. I knew I couldn't say no, as I had buggered off and fallen asleep again last night and not seen him.

34B to 36DD

I kid you not. Do you want to know how you too can achieve this? Remember I told you about the first guinea-pigologist I saw four years ago? The one who mentioned in passing the ten-year change process...IN PASSING, AS IF IT WASN'T THAT BIG A DEAL.

One paragraph in and I'm ranting already. Anyway, he prescribed estradiol transdermal gel and told me to use it on my legs once a day. I duly trotted off to the pharmacy and bought a tube; and all the other 6 tubes remaining in stock; in case they ran out. It is Dar es Salaam after all. I had to go to the cash point for the second lot, as they cost lots of USDs.

I rushed home to apply it and waited. It seemed that within about half an hour, my boobs took on a life of their own and were straining at my bra. Fuck though, the pain was tremendous. I had to wear my maternity bra in bed – (imagine bringing your maternity bra with you in your container from the UK)? Well, I say it was a good thing I did.

If my daughter touched me anywhere between my tummy button and my neck it was so sore. Cuddling was like torture. Going to bed was torture, breathing was torture. Being was torture. My boobs were rock hard, huge and agony. I thought I must have used too much, so I assumed that if I used less, it would be fine. In hindsight, the words – very stupid – come to mind, but at the time I never thought to go back to the doctor.

I carried on for 2 weeks. then I FINALLY called the guinea-pig-ologist. Only he wasn't there. My main man who said he would be available to monitor me when I really needed it wasn't around. Not only was he not around, he was not in Dar, he was in the UK, having surgery as he was elderly and had in fact retired. I went to the "ordinary" doctor, who said "oh dear", we will pass on the information. I never heard from either of them again.

This was the beginning of my interaction with front line medical services in relation to being peri-menopausal.

I stopped the gel, my boobs went back to normal and I was able to breath, work, walk, cuddle and go to bed and carry out other activities that ordinary people engage in during the course of an average day. But I still had all the peri-menopausal symptoms.

By the way, if anyone needs any estradiol transdermal gel I still have 6 tubes of the stuff, complete with the little plastic measuring applicator device, which is unfortunately not very precise.

There is no rush, they expire in about 2084.

From M&M&Ms to the Gym

I can't believe I've only just noticed that menstruation; miscarriage and menopause all begin with M. I know you thought chocolate. Much more pleasant, I do agree. Interesting how nobody talks about any of them much. All to do with women's bodies. I think I'm onto something here.

But not today, I Can't Be Bothered – CBB. Have you heard of that? It is the polite version of CBA; I will leave you guessing on that one, till tomorrow or when I remember to tell you.

No. Today I want to tell you about what happened at the gym yesterday. First you have to understand, if you are not a gym bunny, you don't mess with someone else's floor space. NEVER. That means you cannot be a space invader. If you do by accident, because you are doing a high kick or moving forward or back, you must immediately apologise and then get back in your own spot. If you are a high-level gym bunny, like me, then you wouldn't of course do that, but a lot of "them" are average.

Yesterday something catastrophic happened. There was a jumping bean in the class. It must have happened by accident. I swear she must have been there by mistake, thinking it was a nightclub and I also swear she was still on something. She barely made contact with the ground. I have only seen Maasai's jump higher. Worse she was knocking into people. ME INCLUDED.

Now, this is where the bloody peri-menopause comes in. Mornings are not great for me before 10am. I know I use menopause, peri-menopause and all those words interchangeably, but you know what I mean. I am waiting for the tablets to kick in; I have been up since 5am or earlier. Possibly 3am or 4am – waiting for it to be 5am. Worried I will sleep in and not have my daughter ready for her 6.15am pick up, or worse that I fail to collect the raft of other children, when it is my turn for school pick-up.

ANYWAY, back to the gym – the above was necessary for background to understand my mood.

Well, not quite back to the gym, I had forgotten to change my patch. I have a little alarm that goes off to tell me to change it every 3 days. Problem is, it went off when I was in the car the day before yesterday. I should carry them with me, but I don't and of course I had completely lost it by the time I got home. 24 hours later, holy crap – my patch. I only remembered because I was talking about a patchwork quilt. I need a better patch reminder back up system. My husband has filled my phone and computer with alarms and reminders and asked if a 5-minute warning before I had to take a pill was ok. I need a reminder about the reminder. I have confidence he will sort.

However, a missed patch is a depletion of hormones by 24 hours and that has an impact for 48 hours. I think you are probably getting the picture. I was already incredibly grumpy, fire breathing actually. You may also be thinking that I am dis-organised and stupid and bring many unnecessary mood swings on myself. I agree totally with you on that. I get on my own nerves so much.

While we are on the subject. I had also run out of my darling Xanax. They sound like something from star trek. They are better though than something green and yucky from outer space. They are given to lots of woman to "smooth" out "those" moods. I thought I had another packet in my bathroom drawer but didn't. It was scary to see the reaction I had when I suddenly had less in my pm dose than I was supposed to and no morning tablet at 6 am as usual. I had a cloth brain, ok I'm used to that, but it was much worse than usual. The withdrawal side effects of just a small, missed dose – half a gram, also meant I had no messages from my brain to my arms and legs and felt terribly faint.

NOW, all of you will know, that messages from brain to limbs is quite important for a good gym session; and for the rest of the day's activities as well, for that matter; like driving and well things like sentence construction. The latter is rather less life threatening than the former.

So, you have the picture, as soon as we started class, I was struggling. Mind you, in my defence, I was struggling in my own space. Under "my" fan, which, through years of practice, I can shunt other women away from. Glaring and doing kicks rather close to them – controlled – are two of my methods.

Then SHE appeared. She elbowed me, I was instant aggression, "be careful" I threatened in a low voice and glared at her. She just giggled. I realised she was a complete nutter and off her trolley. She was also young and sweet and had no fucking clue about gym etiquette. She literally must have travelled from the back to the front of the gym space diagonally, getting in everyone's way and utterly oblivious to it all. And, seemingly to the effects of what her own limbs were doing, they were completely independent to her HQ. (Brain).

This wasn't just a case of an irksome beginner going left when everyone goes right, and coming dangerously close to you. Those kinds of beginners know their place and stay at the back. No, she was different. She reminded me of the first wedding dance floor scene in "Four Weddings and a Funeral" when the handsome Scot says something like, "the first time I saw XX – can't remember his name – dance, I feared lives would be lost". Another image sprang to mind of another of my favourite films, Sliding Doors when lovely Gwyneth Paltrow's ex boyfriend sees her in the pub dancing after a rowing match, and says " Oh my god, she is in there having some sort of sponsored epileptic fit."

Do you get the picture?

I was so happy though, because I didn't slap her, push her or do anything to her, that I might have done pre-HRT. At water break, I made myself go and ask her if she was ok and smiled at her. Not a grimace, an actual smile. She had a sore leg and had pulled a muscle. Not surprising really as her legs were flicking up round her head, in moves I had never seen before. The teacher didn't go near her and suggest she tone it down. Maybe he feared for his life.

I was looking for the good.

However, I couldn't cope with my own body and its delayed lack of reactions, so I gave up after 45 minutes and left for a lie down.

The Gym Bunny Returns

Having had 2 bad gyms days because of dosage problems,

my arms, legs and brain connections were back with a vengeance today. Hurrah!

I couldn't believe it though. SHE was also back. It was a step class, with weights. Holy Smoke – even more accessories for her to turn into dangerous weapons. I was wrong though, having a step meant she stayed in front of it and didn't wander off. Brilliant.

As for the weights, well she only dropped them – both – once. Yes simultaneously but they were light. The floor remains intact to live for another fabulous class tomorrow.

Feeing human and pleasant I even asked her how her leg was.

I saw the good.

Big Boobs to Big Bum

Well, some interesting tit bits to share. One was from a friend who asked me would she get the menopause as she is on the pill. What a good question. I don't know. She then told me that one of her friends had decided to stay on the pill till she was 90 just to avoid anything – menopause, ageing etc. Sounds brilliant to me. Head down and keep taking the tablets.

I went to see the new doctor in Dar about IT and she put

me on the contraceptive pill to even out my darling little moods swings. Unfortunately, what it did to me was make me a big, fat bastard – overnight, just like my boobs with the gel. I couldn't believe it; I had to wear tents as nothing fitted. My bum was huge. If you say that with a Scottish accent it is better and more dramatic.

I am not being size-ist, BUT if you are used to being 55 kgs your entire adult life, then it comes as a bit of a shock when you suddenly gain 10kgs with no warning.

I went back saying I couldn't bear it, I was fat and horrid and still not sleeping.

So bugger me, she gave me another contraceptive pill, swearing that it wouldn't make me put so much weight on, and that, the one she had given me was known to make you a fat bastard. Apparently it is the one doctors always start you with just in case it works.

I tried that pill and was still a BFB. Just fat and no pleasanter, this was NOT a good deal. I then got another pill; a pill-lite even – that I would NEVER be a BFB with. But, it was ghastly; side effects galore, sore everything, like PMS all the time. What WAS the point? I persevered thinking that she must be right because she was a doctor and I wasn't. How programmed we are.

A YES Voter – Go Scotland!

A complete diversion. I hope everyone has been closely following this incredible process of grass roots democracy in action. It is fabulous the way that this debate about the UK has developed. It is SO long overdue as far as I am concerned. It links to many elements; the reform of the House of Lords, the overhaul of the Monarchy, federalism. Other countries have overtaken the UK in terms of transforming their systems of government, take South Africa for example. This is when I feel embarrassed that the UK; as an advanced democracy with a lot to showcase which is great; has got behind the curve. We are behind the French. Today is Friday and so all the little darling French children in France and in the French education system globally; are on page 15 of their maths books and all wearing blue t-shirts. In France, they have a federal system, and they kicked the monarchy out some time ago didn't they?

I do feel disappointed, as I really did think that Scotland would do it, but I AM excited by the thought of the Scots having led the way in expressing a strong desire for change of the status quo in the UK as a whole.

I was involved with the Westminster Select Committee for International Development after the Southern Africa Food Crisis in hmm can't remember the exact date. I don't want to lose track as I only have power and therefore Internet for about 30 more seconds. I will get back to you on dates etc. We submitted our own report and also commented on the report submitted by the UK HMG on what they would be doing differently in the next food crisis.

Yes, yes I have been very gainfully employed doing important things for many years. I haven't spent that long lounging around moaning about my body parts, I promise. INGOs – (international non-governmental organisations) were keen to make sure that the Department for International Development DID follows up what they had signed up to. I asked the Chair of the Select Committee, (I can't remember his name now). WHAT the parliamentary monitoring mechanism to ensure departmental compliance and accountability was?

OMG have you noticed how I just slipped into all the jargon?? Well, I learned that there wasn't a monitoring system –

Nothing

NOT even a BAD one.

Once reports are in and submitted, all the select committees move onto their next task. SO the departments could in theory completely take the piss and do nothing. I have to dash and do that bloody bridge again to collect my tiny angel. And NO I still haven't repaired the aircon.

Comments

My blogs are appealing to my friends, family and also occult, porn and SEO sites.

I wonder what it is about the words darling and menopause that make this the case? I really have no answer to that, as there really is nothing remotely sexy about the peri-menopausal decade – PMD. It gets SO tiring writing peri-menopausal decade that it has to be abbreviated from now on.

The occult – well to be fair, being IN the PMD, could be enough to encourage a nice girl to turn to anything that might help with insomnia.

No Wedgie Worries

"Featuring a silicone gripper edge that keeps your suit in place" from Speedo Girls. Have you ever heard of anything more hilarious? This label was taken from a friend's 5-year olds new swimming costume.

You see even if you are IN the PMD, you can still remain light and maintain a sense of humour. I couldn't believe this was now a feature of swimwear. Humans can now even control wedgies? The label is now on my phone.

Got the Date

Just googled myself and found the date of the Southern African Food Crisis I was talking about last week. It was 2002.

Since then there have been several more food crises. East Africa and Somalia are still in the grip of them as I write, as is Africa south of the Sahel. In Somalia there already been SIXTEEN warnings of a crisis waiting to happen. The food security and early warning systems are just archaic.

The Pill Period

Like the painters.

In 2012 and 2013 I was on different contraceptive pills and my darling moods didn't alter much. Then, I was SO, SO lucky to meet MY friend. She was hilarious, and shallow, with hidden depths. My perfect chum. Unknown to me at the time, she was also a secret tablet guzzler.

I had no idea she was peri-menopausal, but when we DID discuss IT; furtively at first and more vigorously from then on; WOW it was another world. I had a partner in crime.

She told me that she had been given anti-anxiety/depressants for mood swings. This I now understand, is common. The little darling white tablets were called Ciprolax. I trotted off to the doctors with my words ready; not the fanny doctor; the other one. He explained that this tablet was meant to take the edge off anxiety, as mood swings started. I couldn't wait to get going with them. Within 10 minutes of taking the first one, I wasn't sure where the ground was in relation to my feet. It was fabulous once I had learnt not to fall over.

Within 2 weeks it was great, I was just floaty enough to sort of get through the day without yelling, tiny downside, terribly forgetful. Can you imagine what it was like living with me, working with me, just being with me? Scary, very scary.

Dates and Diaries

So where was I – oh yes – the pill period. It is quite good trying to remember which tablet was when in the overall ghastliness of the last three years.

Hmmm. So I was on a pill-lite and taking little darling Ciprolax "mood smoothers". I was due a trip to the UK and went to see the GP there. Having consulted with my UK adviser, my older sister, on what I should be taking.

I still can't believe I didn't go to a guinea-pigologist. I think it was because I didn't want to see a man. I still thought there were only male gynaecologists.

Why ARE men guinea-pigologists? Isn't that weird and kinky? I didn't want my tackle being looked at by a random man. My little sister recommended her guinea-pigologist, but he was a bit far from where I was staying. She even suggested I email him. My tackle could not have been safer than email she assured me. I didn't do that. I still thought that I only needed primary care services.

After a standard 5-minute consultation, the GP in the UK put me on Ellesse Duet. It was fabulous and I instantly lost all the weight I had put on.

I was now thin but mean.

The Ciprolax had stopped working.

Thin And Mean

I think it should be lean and mean but there we go.
So there I was coming back to Dar August 2013 with new HRT.

Wearing my own clothes, which fitted, taking my Ciprolax every day until….

I noticed that I wasn't completely ok, despite all the tabs.

The HRT stopped the migraines – tick and a gold star.

The HRT stopped the weight gain – tick and a gold star.

The HRT didn't stop my mood swings – big fucking cross

The HRT didn't stop my insomnia – big fucking cross

On balance a bit better but still quite crap.

Oh yes and my business was expanding and so very stressful. I didn't mention that did I? It was due to expand and then close to a very tight deadline.

So back to the doctor with, "I can't sleep and I am a fire breathing monster". "Ok", says he, "I will give you Xanax to help you deal with the immediate anxieties and you can reduce it when you have sorted out your business".

I was then on HRT, and two different types of anti-anxiety tablets. Are you keeping up? Good, just checking.

I floated through some of last year very nicely on this upgraded version of Valium. I think a strip of them should be in every girl's handbag. When I was particularly forgetful on my old HRT, and couldn't count; my very lovely friend always had some for me if I had run out. Especially on Sundays and at events when I suddenly realised I couldn't guarantee that I could control myself.

What more could a friend do than share her last few Xanax's?

Sunday lunches for example when we were all out; would became highly stressful events for me if we didn't get the order in quickly enough. The drinks order would be all wrong, the children's food order would be all wrong. Whingy, hungry children – not good.

Once she asked me if I had taken a tab as I was getting VERY visibly twitchy and grumpy.

"No" I replied, "I didn't think I needed them at the weekends."

"You must", she insisted, "weekends are very stressful. For these sort of events, I can't get through them otherwise". She slipped one to me under the table.

I had never thought of it. She was SO right, 15 minutes later I didn't care who was eating what as long as I got my gluten-free pizza.

"It Will All Be Fine In 20 Years…"

My friend's mother said that she had much more energy in her 60s and 70s, than she had had in her 50s. That is such a great, cheery thought isn't it? I am nearly 54 so not much longer then.

By "coming out" that I am menopausal, it is first interesting to watch people's reactions and second great to hear all the stories from women of different ages. Older women recount the secrecy and depression and the relief of finding others who were going through THE DECADE. Younger women in their 40s are shocked that it is a DECADE and really don't know what will hit them – poor darlings. Even younger ones in their 30s remember their mothers having IT and without exception, their mothers being quite mad. Mood swings are UP there as a major feature.

Looking back now, I realise that my mother also seemed to be quite potty at times. Alternately yelly and lovely. That is so familiar these days for me; but at the time I thought she was just ghastly. As my daughter does with me. The only thing that is better is that I am more informed and therefore so is my daughter. The yelling is the same though. Better though now as I take my tablets regularly, aided by my phone, which beep alarms and reminders at me all day so I don't forget.

I remember my mother muttering from time to time; "I won't let "them" put me on Valium for three years and end up like Auntie Ida".

"Who's them, mum?" I recall asking. "Doctors, male doctors, that's what they do to women", she replied with some vigour. Well now I think maybe Auntie Ida had the better deal and floated through her decade. I certainly wouldn't blame her.

Cold Turkey

I recommend that you don't try this at home.

What a disaster. Having brought 6 months worth of HRT back from the UK, I found them at the Oyster Bay chemist. I live a hand to mouth; always running out of tablets; sort of existence and so never bought 6 packets or anything like that.

Imagine my horror, when I went to the chemist when I had taken my LAST tablet only to be told that they had run out.
"Run out", I squeaked, 'what do you mean? Will you have some more tomorrow?"

"No Madame, we don't know when more will come".

I called for reinforcements – husband – and first had to confess that I had run out of HRT. I then explained that life would be catastrophic for ALL of us, if I stopped taking them just like that from one day to the next. He got the message. He asked me what the chemical compounds were in the tablets.

"What"? I asked, I thought he was joking. "I have no

idea". "Well find out," he said.

I looked it up for the first time since I had started taking them. I have always been a head in the sand kind of gal. Never read anything when I was pregnant as it all sounded very unpleasant. Didn't WANT to know what I was taking to get through my PMD.

He went to lots of different chemists and drew a blank in each. Finally he found Ellesse Solo, he had found – would that do?

"Yes', I said gratefully and took a tablet. The Ellesse bit was the same; it was just the darling little Solo bit that was different to the Duet bit.

Flying Solo

Well of course the Duet and Solo are there for a reason after Ellesse, which after all is only a brand name.

Within 12 hours I felt really shocking, it is hard to describe over-dosing on a hormone but it is something akin to having barbed wire scraping through all your veins and arteries throughout your entire body. Well I did finally read the packet, thank god you all say.

Solo by definition means one. It therefore was supposed to be taken with another hormone replacement. I stopped after taking 2 tablets on 2 consecutive days. It still means that it is another 3 days before the barbed wire leaves your body. I don't know where it goes.

So then I really was cold turkey with just my darling anti-depressants as back up. It was April 2013.

I had to get to June 13th when I went to the UK to get more HRT. This time I WAS going to a guineapig-ologist.

Abandoning The Bridge

Hurrah! My daughter has a place on the school bus. I do feel guilty but the relief out weighs it tenfold. Out of 10 trips, I now only do 3. Admittedly they are all in the afternoon and so at the hottest time, however that is a small price to pay. I can now work from 6.30am till 8.30am and again after the gym from 11.00 till 14.00pm. That is a 5-hour working day. It is SO short compared with any other working day I have had since I was 21. In early September, I actually felt lazy, so I had to give myself quite a SERIOUS talking to.

My big focus is HEALTH as well as work for the rest of the year, the rest of my life actually.

That sounds very dramatic. I clearly don't have a dramatic bone in my body; BUT I have learnt that all your girly hormones, which protect you from cancer and heart disease etc., simply stop that protection during the PMD as the darling hormones diminish.

PLUS any family history medical time bombs you may have; and been ignoring or unaware of; can start rearing their heads. Just about now I would say.

Where do the wonderful, good hormones go I wonder? Is there a hormone heaven? A special cloud where they all retire to and look down at us gals struggling along without them? Or are they recycled? I wonder.

Google Search

Who exactly invented Google search? Should I know? Was it a bearded chap from California? I love them whoever they are. They are how I found MY guinea-pig-ologist's clinic. It was true to say that I was in a bit of a state when I loaded myself onto the plane in June. I had been guzzling Xanax as my new alternative self – prescribed drug of choice to replace my rapidly diminishing hormones. Trouble is though, they are not gender specific. I did offer them to my husband once, so you see – they can work for everyone. They are a bit like the proverbial blunt instrument. THAT I realised is the issue with the PMD. Why did it take me three years to realise? Well I can't say, but we are all different. I know such a short sentence yet so profound. My symptoms were different to other women's. One friend started having very irregular and heavy periods. This became somewhat of a liability as you can imagine, on the train going to work. She had to start carrying extra clothes with her. She also had visible hot flushes about every 20 minutes. I have never had either of those symptoms. I have had ALL the others. My hot flushes sneak up on me at night time, little bastards. Having decided I couldn't leave my father's postcode area, I googled lady gynaecologists with my postcode. Up SHE popped or rather her clinic did. What sealed the deal for me was the list of symptoms and issues. I then read the history of the clinic. SHE had set it up as SHE had felt that there was a gap in services for women in the PMD. Too bloody right I thought. They had a Q&A. I think it was especially designed for me. One of them was; do you find it hard at 9am and 5pm? I gasped – they knew! There was also an elegantly diplomatic sentence about GPs needing more support to deal with the differences in symptoms and tailor them to specific women and to link it into family history and risk profiling. I didn't even know her but I loved her as well. I rushed to tell my father that it wasn't my fault I was horrid. Poor man he has a wife and THREE daughters. Even the dog was a girl. Can you imagine the hormone excesses and depletions he has dealt with in his lifetime?

The Dream

"Call security quick…" A siren went off. Two burly men came into the room. They grabbed me. "Lavender doesn't work", I yelled at the guineapig-ologist. "Hot baths and a glass of warm milk don't work either." "It's been three years I can't try lavender and come back in 3 months… I need something stronger NOW, I want to get some sleep like other people". I was screaming at her and trying to hit her. I woke up. It was 2am. I was shortly due to go for a Well Woman Clinic appointment. Well at 16.00pm. I couldn't get back to sleep – would you be able to? I got up and had some warm milk; no just kidding; I had a cup of coffee. The dream showed my levels of anxiety around the possibility that she might not take me seriously. I got my list ready, and then re-did it, at least three more times, trying to be as concise as possible. I needed a potted history of what I had been on and how I had reacted to each different med and what my current symptoms were. I got my opening lines ready so she knew the deal:

I had felt terrible for three years.

I had to be able to work.

I had to be able to sleep.

I had to be able to be pleasant to those around me, especially my child.

Lavender and hot milk were not options.

In other words; DON'T FUCKING MESS WITH ME

Waiting For The Appointment

I made my husband come with me; I was so worried I might hit her if she said something that wasn't what I wanted to hear. The administration of her office was terrible. I had managed not to "email-rant" too much as I got the appointment and didn't get replies or clarity as to address etc. It was fucking private for god's sake my PMD side "said to self". I remembered what it was like in Dar and so sucked it up. When we got to the office, I was in a complete state. But not in so much of a state that I didn't notice the chintz curtains and plumped up cushions. The waiting room was what I imagined a modern mental home would be like; light muzak playing; everything soothing and calming – all designed for mad women at the end of their tether clearly.

I had to fill in a form with 6 sections. For all of them, I ticked severe. Except for the box about facial hair. I asked my husband, "Have I got facial hair"? "Yes", he said, "just joking, no you don't". He peered at me, "no you don't". Great one box I could tick no. The form was whisked away from me. We waited. I tried to breath properly. I had been doing neck breathing all day. I thought I would pass out if I tried breathing into my diaphragm.

The Actual Appointment

"Can you come with me"?

A jolly voice beckoned me out of the waiting room. It was HER, not a nurse nor an admin officer but her, the woman who I had been hitting in my dream.

I was speechless and terrified. Both were rare feelings for me, but I was. My husband followed behind me, feeling rather out of place in all the chintz. I trotted after her, saying; "I thought I should bring my husband", and saying to myself – "I am paying for this, I am not 15, get a grip woman".

We all sat down. She had a computer print out on her desk. I stared at her. She opened, as clearly I wasn't able to, "well, you are in a bad way, aren't you?"

That was it. The relief was palpable. My husband noticeably relaxed, he has been seriously concerned that he would need to protect the doctor from me. I think that was why he had worn his special power training shoes and a comfy "action" shirt; worn out in case of; well action.

I then gave her my list I had honed down. She agreed with everything and everything she said was music to my ears. It is strange how often you can't remember very important things as you are in a pickle.

Some of the things I remember her saying;

It is good you came now,

You have severe symptoms because of your family history kicking in, diabetes and heart disease

You do have to think of your family, your child will remember,

SHE TOOK ME SERIOUSLY

I started to write down all she told me. She stopped me and said she had a sheet.

Every sentence was a joy. I WAS a mess but she could sort me out. She told me this, that and the other. I muttered at my husband, are you getting this? I could only remember one sentence until another replaced it. She was eloquent and it all made perfect sense. She took most of my blood for various tests and then looked at my tackle. I didn't even mind that. "Oh yes", she said as she peered.

"Poor you".

I left clutching a large paper bag of pills and patches, instructions and daily charts to fill in. My head was reeling. We had a teleconference on the Friday; it was now Monday; and we would Skype monthly from Tanzania. We went to the reception, where I parted with vast amounts of cash, filled in more forms and left.

The Hunt Is On

"Is this the tablet we had to go round the country to find for you mum"? We were leaving the next day to return to Dar. I had now run out of Xanax, I had been taken much higher doses on holiday, as it was all deeply unrelaxing. Oh no, I did my usual of taking my last one, before checking if I had more. I called HER. She said her pharmacy would issue the prescription and we could collect it.

PHEW. No, not that easy, even in the UK. Hubs with kids went to collect prescription from private clinic on the other side of the town. They wouldn't give it to him, as he wasn't me. They were nervous, as it is strong. "She has been taking it for ages," he shared. "She knows all about it".

Not sure if that was the best line.

They decided they needed to speak to me. They couldn't get through they told him. Where was I? At my father's. On the loo, in the garden – who knows? I called them back immediately. I got an answer machine. I called reception I got an answer machine. I called husband. One of the kids answered, "we got the prescription, and we're shopping and will get it later". And then hung up. FIVE hours later they turned up, brandishing the familiar white paper bag with the "gold bars" inside. They had tried 6 different places and ended up finally getting them in

Tesco up the motorway. I felt so bad for them. It was LOVE, wasn't it? Or at least the knowledge that it was equally in THEIR interests that I had that tablet that day, if they wanted their own lives to be worth living. When we were back in Dar, I collected my daughter and told her we were nipping to the pharmacy, as I needed to get some more Xanax. "Is this the tablet we had to go round the country to find for you mum"? "Well yes, but county not country". "It felt like the country to us," she replied. "Fair enough", I agreed. Who was I to be so pedantic, with my little knightette in shining armour?

After The Appointment

It was as if she had joined up the dots. Linking precursors to family history with actual symptoms I had by diagnosing based on test results and analysis. I skipped into the car feeling so much lighter. The key for me was first being taken seriously; but more importantly was the fact that SHE had not compartmentalised my head, body and tackle. SHE had looked at the whole picture. I had several calls to make. 2 friends and several family members were waiting with baited breath. First my father, then mother in law, then sisters; the list went on. Little daughter was anxiously waiting with grandpa. She had never known BOTH parents go off together to an appointment with the doctor. I started the tablets immediately. I was conscious that my husband, father and daughter were watching me closely for signs of instant character upgrade. The next morning my mother in law called, "how was I?" SHE HAD said that it would take till at least October to feel more balanced, what with adjustments to the dosage of the patch and the tablets in tandem to a reduction of the "other" tablets. It had to be done slowly and carefully. Of course it did. Only I couldn't wait.

Overdose

I was very lucky I thought. I had finally been to the right doctor. I had the cutest people around me, willing me on. There were no secrets with THIS issue that was for sure. They all knew about the dream, they all knew I needed back up so I didn't cause any damage. It was all going to be fine. Tiny problem. On the sheet SHE gave me for dosage, she wrote 1-2mg of the table Climaval. To my recollection she didn't expressly say start with 1mg and then increase when I tell you. I would have followed those instructions. I was so keen to feel better and nicer, that I took 2mg. That was Monday, by Wednesday I felt terrible. I called her; "no problem", she said soothingly, "you are sensitive so reduce to 1mg". I did, but as you know from before, increasing and decreasing hormones takes time, and it is a bit like turning a large ship round. I was experiencing the symptoms of "over-oestrogenisation."

All the plans I had for the final week were off. I was

"tankered" while I went 360 degrees. Hubs was understandably annoyed. "NO MORE OVERDOSING" he yelled. "I am in charge of hormone dosage". My people had to do the packing while I wafted around. My people also made sure I got on the right plane, even though they may have wished otherwise.

Internet Search With Caution

On the PMD – don't do it; unless you really, really have to; or are a sadist. I have always taken a head in the sand approach to ghastliness in relation to bodily functions. The best and only way as far as I am concerned. I did make the mistake of looking up my meds I was on last week. JUST so I could get the names right for the blog. The information is contradictory, that is why I hate reading about them. One jolly medical menopause site says oestrogen only tabs are high risk for heart disease. Fine, all you have to do is go to the gym for at least 4 hours a day to counteract that.

Then another of the darling medical menopause sites said the opposite; oestrogen only tabs protect you from breast cancer BUT does that mean you will still die of heart disease? The list of side effects covers absolutely everything including sneezing and shopping. The latter is highly dangerous and life threatening. Side effects also seem to include all the 50 PM symptoms. How are you supposed to know what is a symptom and what is something you are about to die of? HOW? Anyway obviously I couldn't sleep last week.

I want to, no I NEED to be awake when the stroke starts, so I can bitch slap it into submission.

In summary, all tablets you take have the potential to kill you.

"Love Hurts, Love Scars, Love Wounds And Mars"

When I saw the title Love Hurts in a menopause blog, I thought YES, great song by great Scottish band Nazareth. NO WRONG, COMPLETELY WRONG – Read on; Menopause Mondays: Love Hurts. How to Cope with Painful Sex During Menopause. There's actually a medical term for this painful intercourse: dyspareunia.

HOW do you even pronounce "that dys" word? We are not going there today or any day – no bloody way. Then another article caught my eye before I went off to eat chocolate to recover from my shock: *Larger Skirt Sizes May Increase Breast Cancer Risk by 33%*. What wearing them, looking at them or just thinking about large skirts? I need to know urgently, as I haven't been able to get images of large skirts wafting about on their own, out of my head since I read that. Oh happy PMD days.

Waiting For Facial Hair

Think it is about number 28 on the TOP 40 yummy symptoms of PM....

I'm waiting.

It's 8.08am I am still waiting. I don't think today is the day.

I will look again tomorrow.

How often do you have to check I wonder?

Have You Heard The Ones About The ...

Q: What's the difference between a pit bull and a woman in menopause?

A: Lipstick

Q: What's 10 times worse than a woman in menopause?

A: Two women in menopause.

The One Eyed Monster

Today is Wednesday. Congratulations, you say I did get the day of the week correct. This makes a change. To be fair to me, though I haven't made any day errors since…. hmm I was going to write last week, but I double booked yesterday evening. Moving on swiftly. So this is Yoga day as well as aerobics. At 9.45am, I was so busy imagining a lie down, that I simply couldn't bring myself to do even one more abdominal crunch. By 9.50am, I had a plan, I had decided I was going to scarper, before the yoga teacher got to the gym and therefore wouldn't see me. Sometimes it is hard to believe that I am 53 nearly 54, and not 10 and constantly in trouble at school. I had my shopping list in my head and thought if I do yoga and shopping that leaves very limited time for lying down before I collect my daughter. My days are governed by how soon I can get home and lie down again. I left class just when the fabulous instructor was doing a torturous exercise, which I decided I didn't need to do, and prepared my escape.

Busted.

There she was as I got downstairs. "Morning, see you in a minute" she called out to me merrily. Back up I trotted, avoiding the instructor whose class I had just left. I had mouthed to him as I had headed for the door, "I have to go to work". What a fibber. Yoga was wonderful, it always is. It was also absolute HELL on this earth. SO,

SO painful, although I am fit now, I am as stiff as an old board and only do neck breathing. I haven't breathed from my diaphragm since well 1900 and ....I am far too highly strung for that. We were doing these extended hip stretches. I know they will be good for me when I finish, but fuck, are they sore when you are in the middle of them.

I also manage to get myself in a pickle with the devil/angel conversations I have. Angel self is in a meditative state breathing into my stretch. Have you seen that happen? Have you? It doesn't exist; it is called grunting with pain, masked as breathing into your stretch. Devil self is running through the shopping list, and added digestive biscuits to it to make a cheesecake. After that I skipped off literally, and DID go to the shops. It was so successful, I think because of yoga. I DID have my list, as it is now on my phone, but I didn't have my glasses so I couldn't see it. However I just went aisle by aisle trying to remember everything. That is quite a dangerous way to shop frankly but I didn't have any temper tantrums or abuse anyone or get grumpy with the fact that the oatcakes are still not there. I even remembered the nutella.

I got home feeling good and smug. First thing the housekeeper says to me was, "mama, we need toilet paper". Had I bought toilet paper? Of course I bloody hadn't.

The One Eyed Monster – Take Two

I completely forgot the one eyed monster bit. I was so carried away with yoga and shopping. Quick before I forget again…. I went to a workshop on Tuesday morning at my daughter's school. We had had a bit of a scramble to get there that morning. I put my mascara and lipstick in my handbag, as I hadn't managed to sort myself out before I left.

Usually I drop her at the bus with scary hair, which has been attacked by the hair pixies in the middle of the night. I have even been known to leave the house at 6.15am with caterpillar breath as well. YUK.

The dogs delayed us. They love coming in the car so much. They are our own personal security detail. They have their own places, one in the front seat, one on the back seat and one in the boot. Unfortunately on this occasion, they couldn't stay in the car while I was at the workshop. I explained it to them, but you know, they just wouldn't listen. By the time we got one out of the car, another one had hopped in. Little monkeys.

Then there were the traffic jams. I did my mascara on one eye, while I was waiting at the first one and put my lip salve on. My daughter did her sunblock and then her mosquito repellant. We then moved off, at the next jam, I put my lipstick on.

When we parked, my daughter left me, as I had to text my husband about something urgent to do with the house, power or water or something. I went off to her classroom, chatted to her and her friend, talked to her teacher and then headed off to the staffroom for the meeting. The presenter started. Suddenly I thought in panic.

I think I only have mascara on one eye. I turned to the woman sitting next to me and whispered, " sorry to bother you, but do only have mascara on one eye?" "Yes," she whispered back helpfully, "have you got an eye infection?" "No," I muttered, "I am menopausal."

SAM is Satisfying Women Everywhere

Look at this wonderful advert. SAMIS SATISFYING WOMEN EVERYWHERE if you have Light Bladder Leakage (LBL), it's time you met SAM (Super Absorbent Material). Designed to lock away wetness better than period pads and liners, you'll find SAM in the full line of Poise products. Now you know what to do if you find yourself starting to have LBLs.

9 Minutes 32 Seconds per KM

The voice came from my bum. Or rather the phone in my bum pocket. I was doing an amazing 9.32/KM. Even the lady in my phone counting my steps seemed impressed. I am in training for the Kilimanjaro Marathon in March. So far, I am on 4 kms walking on flat ground. I'm taking it in stages. Last Sunday it was 12 minutes/KM. That was because between us we had 3 dogs and 3 children. Doing it on my own was fabulous and so fast, but it was for a different reason. I won't bother to keep track on Sundays from now on, as it is cute with the children.

Chake Chake Street is gorgeous. At this time of year it is full of flowers and blossoms. It is also full of people walking, jogging, running and cycling. A lot of them look roughly my age. Anytime you read or look up ANYTHING for the 50 plus age group, it is HORRID. Don't look; just believe all I write; and do an hour of exercise every day for the rest of your life. Then it will all be fine and dandy. Exercise is always written in small print. I think there should only be leaflets with EXERCISE or DIE; something to really have you take notice. The human body is so forgiving on you in your 20s, 30s and even your 40s, when you abuse it mercilessly. BUT when you hit 50; you start paying for bygone sins. Worse you also have to prepare your body for old age. You actually have to decide; do you want a completely crappy old age, with old lady nappies and dribbling? Or do you want a sprightly old age and croak it, while you are gardening or hiking? Women are SO lucky; we get to have the lady nappies made with SAM to be precise, as well as the dribbling while we have our PMD. Then we have a 20-year gap and start it all over again. HURRAH!

RIP Estrogen and Progesterone

No way, not yet.

No one has yet explained to me how they left.

Bus, train, osmosis, evaporation?

Where are MY hormones?

Do they do shifts and have they jumped into someone else's body?

Awake at 3am AGAIN

Yes I know we've had this before, but I am still awake at bloody 3am, so this is what I have to share.

I hope I don't get busted again by hubs and get taken away from the DVD I want to watch while I sulk. He seems pretty dead to the world. I've finished Game of Thrones or rather I got so bored with the lot of them that I looked up the ending in Wikipedia. I had to know obviously otherwise it would have been very untidy. For years now, since breastfeeding in fact, I don't need to watch all the episodes of each particular series I am on. I just need someone to tell me what happened in that episode. Now GETTING someone to tell you seems to me the same as asking if they can give you ALL their money. First shocked and startled and then the same line, but it will spoil the surprise for you.

NO IT WON'T. It is up to me anyway isn't it? Apparently not. Now thanks to Wikipedia, I can look it all up and not bother when some series get on my nerves. They do a lot now, as I am MENOPAUSAL.

I am feeling it a lot today.

Grumpy as fuck.

I creep out of bed and feel so happy. I have great options, The White Queen and Continents. Both brilliant but I feel the TWQ could go the same way as Game of Thrones and be "wikipedia-ed". Certainly not many gals got to have their glorious peri menopausal decade in those days.

Oh fuck. I can't get the telly to work. With 2 remote controls and 2 different mice and a keyboard for the password, I can't have been wearing the right outfit or standing on my head while I tried. I went back to the bedroom and stood by the bed, willing hubs to wake up. He's usually awake more than me at 3am nowadays. Why not now?

I'm v quiet when I wake up, as I don't usually want to wake him up. He says I am too quiet and that I frighten him by creeping about. "I don't creep", I always protest.

"I just don't slam doors and shine my phone into peoples faces at 2 or 3 in the morning. I simply get up quietly". He also has this knee thing when he bangs the bed each time he gets in. He has been doing it for several years; I don't know why he can't lift his bloody leg higher.

Anyway back to last night or this morning at 3am. I thought he might be awake and could turn the telly on for me. I couldn't tell, so I peeped under the net to see if his eyes were open. I had to get quite close, as I'd taken my glasses off. "Ahh", he yelled.

"Ahh", I yelled back terrified by his yell. "What's wrong", he asked. "Is it burglars"? "No", I said, "Why did you yell"? He asked. "You gave me a fright, when you yelled" I replied.

"I gave YOU a fright, what were YOU doing peering into my face like that. You gave ME a fright. What's wrong with you?"

"I just wanted to see if you were awake and I had to get close as I couldn't see properly".

My daughter came charging into the room, "Mum, dad what's up, I heard yelling, is everything alright? Are the guinea pigs and the tortoise ok?"

I really must learn to turn the telly on by myself.

Morning Briefings Have Ceased

When I closed my business down in August and was no longer working 18 hours a day. I would feel all twitchy when I was starting to write and my hubs would CHAT to me at 6.30am. I had already been up since 5am (or earlier) and dropped my child at school; this was my time to work. Then I realised that I could squeeze him in for a little while, and perhaps SHOULD, as I was always asleep by the time he got back at night by 8pm.

I wasn't used to this, talking about OUR EMPIRE in daylight hours. It was amazing. With three children in three different schools and universities, properties we pretend to own – (darling mortgages), cars needing repairing, issues with the lack of water, issues with power cuts, vermin infestations, rent payments, repairs, insurance renewals, topping up the diesel, holidays.

Suddenly there was a list, which went on and on. Chats went from lists, which went to action points. I tried to cope; after all, we have morning briefings at work, why not for your home life? Yes, but suddenly my morning briefings were getting a bit ONE SIDED.

Well not anymore, I have just put a stop to these morning briefings. It started to leave me with a longer and longer list of things suddenly I had to do, as I had time now.

Holy Fuck and then my daughter started. "Mum can you do... today?" Just like her father, when she got home she would ask me, "have you done what I asked you to this morning"?

My dear hubs encourages my writing and says indeed I must focus on it and in the same sentence adds, it won't take you long to fill up the diesel.

"How do you know, you have never done it?"

Two weeks ago, I burst into tears as you do when you are 54 years old in the fourth year of your peri-menopausal decade. I sobbed and sniffed and explained that I had to go to the gym (exercise or die), and I had to collect our child at 1.45pm everyday. That really didn't leave much time to write and do my work. I couldn't do all those things.

So sweet.

Last Wednesday I started working as soon as I had dropped my daughter. 6.20 am great. I felt a looming presence.

"So sorry", he replied, "I just need to ask you something. I don't want to interrupt you.

"I'm just in the middle of this sentence and I will forget it if I talk"

"No problem, you carry on".

Fantastic. I was on my timer and I made sure we had a chat NOT a list, a CHAT before he left. He had 10 minutes.

You see, I have been so spoilt living overseas. For years, my office would make sure that the house was dealt with so I could do my job. Then when I started my own business at the same time my husband did, we ran out of electricity within 3 days. Neither of us even looked at the meter. Well I did actually; at least I knew where it was. But I didn't have my glasses on and it wasn't on 27kw, which would have got us through the night.

No it was 2.7kw, which didn't.

Hot season 34 degrees at night and no breeze.

I Am Not Asking For A Pedicure

September and the first half of October were bad. I didn't feel any better with all my tablets. Reducing Xanax and having the screaming hab-dabs, every afternoon, resulted in my little girl saying several times she wanted to be adopted out for the afternoons. The doctor here, had said that as I was on HRT, I needed to reduce the anti anxiety tablets.

We had an infestation of bees and rats and so while we were fumigated with all sorts of fabulously strong chemicals, probably illegal in the UK, she went and stayed at a friend's house. She ended up staying the whole weekend as the smell was terrible afterwards and she wouldn't have been able to play in the garden. When she came back, I tried not to, but I just had to ask – "did you miss me, even a tiny bit?" "No", she said from up her favourite tree, "it was great not having anyone yelling at me for two whole days". Fuck.

I also can't believe it took me a whole 4 weeks to get an appointment with the guineapig-ologist in the UK. I was so CROSS. I first waited 1 week just for a reply to my first email with a time slot to talk to her on the phone. This came 7 days later after I had chased it up. My chaser email was irate, but, I like to think on the whole it was measured.

Slightly.

I don't dare look at it, so you will just have to believe me. The response was, "so sorry but all our staff are sick. Oh and by the way, the doctor doesn't do Skype calls with people overseas. I will ask if she is prepared to make an exception". Still no date for a phone appointment.

My interpretation of this was; I will check with someone, who gives a fuck about you, next week Friday, when she comes in, for her part time job share, if she and her extended family are, all feeling ok.

I then replied that the doctor HERSELF had told me she would do Skype calls with me. My second reply was "Thank you for your enquiry. Our emails are checked twice daily and we will respond to you as soon as possible"…

It is impossible to rant at a general email like that. My husband was telling me to phone, but as I felt unstable and very yelly, I didn't think I was safe.

Darling Doctor – get more staff. I am a desperate woman. I have read too much about large skirts, side effects of just about everything resulting in heart attacks and breast cancer to be able to sleep. I have tried to reduce my darling Xanax tablets and am on 1/4 in the mornings and 1/4 at night. I have returned to being a fire-breathing monster in the evenings and DON'T sleep at night. NOT even a TINY bit. I have been laying in wait for my heart attack. I feel nauseous, gaseous – NOT nice for a girl, NOT nice at all, with tingling toes and fingers. Is it diabetes?

Then I sent the killer email. You know the type you should save to draft. The one I would have saved to draft three years ago.

I wrote, I AM NOT ASKING FOR A PEDICURE BUT MEDICAL HELP. I DON'T FEEL WELL.

Insomnia by Day, Sleep by Night

Seems to be no fucking chance for me at the moment.

Why don't we get insomnia in the daytime? It would be so much better. I lay there last night confusing myself trying to add up hours of sleep I would get if I fell asleep immediately. Then 30 minutes later I had to re-calculate. I still have to get up at 5am to get the angel ready for school. I think I should just sleep in my clothes, and she should go to bed in her school uniform, then we could get up at 5.15am.

I LOVE HER

It was still another two weeks before I got to speak to the doctor herself. BUT when I did, it was fabulous. It was like being enveloped by someone who knew what to do and could boss me around. We were on mobiles, as I couldn't hear her on Skype from Tanzania. The line kept breaking up; there was a terrible racket from her end. I explained everything to her, she asked for my little girl's feedback and then swept in with instructions.

I LOVED IT.

The summary was that my hormones were still shot to buggery and I would need a year of "steady ship". She told me to STOP reducing the Xanax, as it was more dangerous to keep fiddling around with different dosages when my hormones were depleted. I had to double the dose of the oral hormones and even triple them as I was on the lowest and I needed more blood tests in December when I was going be in UK. She asked me lots of searching questions about my diet. As I am insulin resistant – I still don't fully understand what that means, I have to have low carbohydrate diet.

She thought my lunches might be turning me into a fire-breathing monster in the afternoons, as well as everything else. She also pointed out that as I am up in the middle of the fucking night to get ready for the school day, that it wasn't surprising I was snookered by 3pm.

Also if you are not getting the right type of sleep, you might as well be awake.

Hurrah -I am still going to be keeping darling Xanax's share levels high!

"I'm too sexy for my shirt, too sexy..."

You all remember that fab song by Right Said Fred? If you are too young, then Google it and watch it on you tube it is brilliant.

Having had my wonderful call with the doctor this morning, I doubled my morning hormones, added another one in at night and upped the Xanax. And, as you know, if you have been reading carefully, with hormones you don't just take one and immediately revert to your former, fabulous self. It takes time. I am really impatient and I wanted my new regime to WORK.

The challenge is that the options seemed to be:

Dopey and pleasant and can only do one thing in a day – courtesy of my darling happy tabs

OR

Be ghastly and get a lot more done in a day – courtesy of not taking my happy tabs.

I put that to my daughter.

Easy she said, "I want you pleasant and get more done in a day".

Well she is only 9.

Back to being sexy. NOT

It was half term and we were on the plane to our mini break in Zanzibar with friends. I was tired. I know what a sur-bloody-prise. In fact I just dropped off. On a small15-seater plane, I usually puke, but I was so tired I fell asleep and got caught in glorious Technicolor gob wide open, head nodding, catching flies pose. We were held in a holding pattern over Stone Town and so the pilot took us on a little tour down the coast.

We were flying over the Indian Ocean, which is SO beautiful. It was so clear they could see whales below us.

Well apparently they could, I was having my nod off. My friends tried to wake me to look at the wonderful view. I remember saying, "leave me alone, I've seen the view". SNORE.

They had to yell to wake me. I really didn't want to get off. I wanted to stay on the plane and fly between Dar and Stone Town all day and get 12 hours sleep. I knew something was afoot; there were too many smiles and giggles. Sex kitten that I am, I came to, wiped away the dribble and got off.

Hurrah for half term but that photo didn't make it to Facebook.

I Should Have Been a Detective

Be honest – how many people know; first where your thyroid gland is and second what it does? I made a fatal mistake yesterday. A HUGE one. I read a book called The Menopause Thyroid Solution by Mary J Shomon. Actually I have to confess that I downloaded it on my birthday, which was Monday. I will leave you to digest that I did that on my ACTUAL birthday.

It was brilliantly written and researched, but of course, the reason I told you never to read anything and stick your heads in the sand like I do, STILL STANDS. Remember exercise or die. That is all you need.

I broke my own rule. Feeling slightly braver, I thought I should be a tiny bit better informed.

Wrong.

My blood test results in August showed that my thyroid level was up. In the covering letter the doctor in UK suggested I take a tablet to bring it to normal. But the GP here told me that the side effects of the tablet were increased anxiety. Now, I don't know, if any of you has the impression that I MIGHT be slightly on the anxious, highly-strung, neurotic side when they dished out personality traits. My sisters and niece and I like to think that we are the "highly-strung XXXX gals". I think on balance, taking a measured approach to this, it would fair to say, that yes, on the whole, I could be going through a period of heightened anxiety, and could do with NOT proactively making it WORSE.

In brief, Holy Fuck, NO, don't take a med that even hints at increasing anxiety.

It has taken me this long to read about my thyroid. All right, first remind myself where it was, I DID know when I was 14,and then read about it, in depth. A summary of my understanding of the book is; peri-menopausal and menopausal symptoms can mask thyroid problems because guess what? Yes, the sneaky little bastard symptoms are the same.

The woman who wrote it makes the VERY IMPORTANT point that most front line GP doctors are not adequately informed about menopause, peri-menopause and the link to thyroid problems and so don't know what tests to order for you. This also goes for all the other yummy things that you need to watch out for during menopause.

So, if the HRT you are on, ISN'T working to bring you back to the planet earth, that is the planet which men, children and young women inhabit; then you need to have more tests and a nice doctor who gives a fuck about women. This caring doctor needs to keep trying to find out what else it might be, AS WELL AS depleted hormones. Don't think for a minute that you get to keep your hormones. Oh no.

All the things I should eat because of being insulin resistant, I shouldn't be eating if I have thyroid problems.

It is all enough to turn a gal to chocolate. Yesterday, I am afraid having delved into that jolly read, been to the gym, felt completely fucked, I stopped at the supermarket and bought a bar of chocolate. This was all by 9am EAT (East Africa Time) when all you UK lot are still in bed slumbering sweetly.

Men, children and young women that is.

Chocolate is NOT on any list – type 2 diabetes, heart disease, thyroid-itis (I think it is called), FB-itis.

But it WAS gluten free.

No SAM For Me

No I don't need SAM – Super Absorbent Material for those LBL moments. Light Bladder Leakage in case you have forgotten.

You know that I love the gym so much. I really, really do. I hate getting there and often for the first 5 minutes, I can be a bit sulky frankly. But when those great hormones hit in, the exercise ones, can't remember what they are called, it is just fabulous. PLUS these little darling, sporty hormones don't disappear like some of the others bloody do.

The other great thing is that I did 90 minutes of super clenches. It is all for the pelvic floor, which is, guess what, another body part that can get quite unruly, if not tightly managed, during your decade of doom. For ordinary walking and daily activities you should just try and clench your pelvic floor as much as you can, without looking or sounding weird. At the gym, you need to super clench for maximum benefit.

Impressed? Super clenches work those little darling muscles, which stop you getting LBLs so that you don't need SAMs.

Freckles Are Great

Well it is just that when I got back from my mini break, all my freckles had popped out. I have that very white, very freckly complexion. I grew up in the Caribbean. Island of Curacao to be precise. SEVEN glorious years. I was a SHELL child. I loved it there, I thought all children grew up on islands and was very surprised to find out when it wasn't the case. We went to the beach every single weekend. My parents did slather cream on, but it was an oily factor 3,or something like that, as they didn't know much about skin cancer back in those days.

Last week, a friend commented; "you look well (after your mini break), I haven't seen you with so many freckles." I simpered. I love my freckles, and thanks to my parents, for always being so positive about them, when they were very much on show when I was young, I have always loved them. They were "special" apparently and only "special" children had them. I was too busy feeling fabulous and never noticed that neither of my sisters had them. Actually come to think of it, no one at school had them either. I really WAS special.

It was not so much, as if I had a huge love affair with them and couldn't stop looking at myself in the mirror; I just wasn't embarrassed at all to have them. While I was a teenager and in my 20s, I never really gave them much thought, until that comment from a friend last week reminded me of my first job overseas, teaching in Sri Lanka.

For once this has NOTHING to do with the menopause, hurrah.

Shortly after I arrived in Sri Lanka, several of my students asked me what the spots were on my face. "Spots", I asked, thinking they didn't have the vocabulary for the CORRECT word.

"No, freckles", I said firmly and wrote it on the board so they even knew how to spell the word correctly. I also pointed to the boy with acne pimples and said "spots" and pointed to my freckles and said "freckles".

I thought that was the end of this little misunderstanding. No.

"Madame, why are your spots always worse on

Mondays?" the bolder ones asked me. They had clearly been discussing my freckles in some depth. Why doesn't Madame Agnes have them?" I went through the whole spots/acne and freckles routine.

Then on that very same day, my colleague said, "I'm so sorry for you".

"Why"? I asked.

"The students have been telling me about your spots".

"Bloody hell", I replied, "don't you start, and they are FRECKLES".

"Yes, I know", she said soothingly, as if I was nuts. Her expression changed, "you must stop eating all that pineapple, it only makes those spots worse you know, and you won't get a good husband".

The Runaway Diaphragm

Why did that suddenly pop into my head? Oh yes, I remember. I was awake at 2am, and for some reason, I was thinking about how extraordinary it is, that a woman can still get pregnant when she is in the throes of being peri-menopausal and even menopausal. As if that wasn't enough to deal with.

From there, I imagined an octopus instead of a baby, as nature might be trying to get you pregnant and then equally trying to stop you. Then I leapt to thinking about all the warnings to continue contraception for a year, I think it is, after your last period, just in case... and the image of a diaphragm came to mind.

Slippery little fuckers aren't they? I could never keep hold of mine long enough for it to be any use to me.

I had a most hilarious session with a health visitor, or is it a family planning visitor, years ago now. It must have been in the UK, where I went to a group briefing on how to use a diaphragm. There was a portable display unit, with LOTS and LOTS of different sized diaphragms. Some were absolutely teeny tiny and others were simply the MOST enormous items, known to womankind, that I had ever seen before or since.

After the talk, we got a 121 with one of the nurses. This was equally hilarious, as you got to practice holding one, putting the cream stuff onto it, and "preparing it for insertion". That meant squeezing the sides of it together to make it narrow enough. I never got to the latter stage because mine simply just kept escaping, flinging itself far across the room... with a will of its own.

For those of you who have never seen one, they are rubbery with a circular covered ring, made of wire or some other very pliable, very bouncy sort of material.

I told a friend about this feisty object. She relayed to me that she had also thought it might be good to try one. She had gone through a similar process to me, but had been more successful, and been allowed to take hers home to "practice" with. Not to use for contraception, you understand, just to practice stage one and two. She would then have to report back 5 days later, and move onto stage three, if she was ready. I think it could take weeks, before you were awarded your own special diaphragm that came in an equally special little plastic holder.

Unfortunately, without the lovely nurse lady to assist my friend, her diaphragm had ended up FLYING right OUT of her hand, the first time she practiced.

It landed on the bathroom ceiling and hung suspended by (far too much) KY Jelly for a few seconds, before plopping merrily onto the bathmat.

The joys and dignity of womanhood.

Destined To Be A Moon Cup Virgin

I am still in shock. Telling my ambulatory diaphragm story last week led a new friend to inform me, that the shenanigans with my diaphragm, had reminded her of her now secret weapon. This secret weapon had first given her problems until she had gained the upper hand in its use and care.

What IS this, you ask?

IT is a Menstrual Moon Cup.

Holy Fuck, I hear you say, either out loud as I did, or to self as you may do.

Yes, holy fuck indeed. I have never heard of them. I, who have lived to the age of 54, have never heard of them.

I looked at the website link she gave me, which you MUST ALL DO. I looked at the small photo in the demonstration video box and thought it looked like a Tupperware, a small one, with no lid. I clicked play. We - my 9 year old and I watched spell bound as she poked and prodded this small rubbery like object, into a variety of positions to show how it worked. It is a plastic tampon with a tube at the bottom so you can haul it out. It looks like a funnel. The sort you use to decant liquids into small containers.

THEN we watched a RAP VIDEO on the same website, with two girl gangs giving out to each other in a public toilet. I think that is the expression to use. Two groups of girls pretending to shout at each other, one gang for tampons and the other group for moon cups. I can honestly swear I have never seen anything like it. We had to use the sub titles, I was too old and my little girl too young, to understand what they were saying. It was Tampons against Moon Cups. There is an excellent environmental case to be made for Moon Cups.

I want one.

But I don't think they will have them in Tanzania. Mind you they are awfully good at ducking and diving here, and making do with odds and ends. I expect if I went into a pharmacy and asked for one, they would probably helpfully point me in the direction of a hardware store to be sold a

Small funnel...

How To Set Fire To Your Moon Cup

My new friend and a very select group of her friends swear by these very Moon Cups, BUT, as I told you, it took her some time to gain the upper hand with hers. I thought you might like the instructions for ONE WAY To Clean a Moon Cup.

To Sterilise Your Moon Cup

Place Moon Cup in a saucepan of boiling water for 5 minutes, preferably on a Saturday, when all your children are home and it is complete madness.

Leave the kitchen immediately you have put the Moon Cup in the water with the gas on, as you forgot to do something urgent for one of your small children.

Leave your second small child, under the age of 10, alone in the kitchen

Allow saucepan to boil dry and set fire to pan, causing large orange flames to sweep across stove top

Train small child, who was left in kitchen, to call out to you, when Moon Cup saucepan is on fire

Dash downstairs swearing

Throw Moon Cup in basin of cold water

Thank small child

Order new Moon Cup

Repeat above process until owner stays in kitchen for the entire 5-minute period without taking their eyes off the pan or uses timer

Coming Out

The Oxford Dictionary definition of 'coming out' is.

In political, casual, or even humorous contexts, "coming out" means by extension the self-disclosure of a person's secret behaviours, beliefs, affiliations, tastes, identities, and interests that may cause astonishment or bring shame.

There are several examples in the dictionary. I have included just a small sample of some of the most hilarious for your reading pleasure:

Coming out as a conservative (I kid you not)

Coming out as multiple (of what I wonder)

Coming out of the broom closet (this is apparently if you are a witch)

And a quote from prominent atheist Richard Dawkins, who states, "There is a big closet population of atheists who need to 'come out.'
NOTHING about menopausal women.

I now refer back to the part of the original sentence – which "may cause astonishment". I made a conscious decision in, I think, September, that when men asked me, what I was doing since I closed my business, I would reply honestly. I just HAD to be able to start saying the M word out loud to strangers, without either wanting to giggle or leave the area.

I have to say two and a half months in, that I have quite a variety of different responses to my outing myself about being menopausal and writing a book about the subject.

Theses responses include; double takes, looking shifty – (not me), swiftly changing subject, asking what the menopause is, and one man who looked at his wife, and said, I think you better read her book.

I have now become braver. I did in fact look shifty the first time I said it, so the above is not quite true. But I NEVER looked as shifty as the men who did. I do still feel the need to add quickly, but it is funny, so you would like it. I am working on slowing down my delivery and not gabbling. I want to get to the stage, where, I can maintain the conversation about it, by asking what they know about their subject, and if there mother or sister or father ever told them anything about it. Work in progress.

It is not just men who look shifty though, I have to say that when I meet women who are complete strangers, they are also a little taken aback. I suppose it depends on the personality as well as the knowledge base. It must be the images of what the menopause conjures up. Periods and messy stuff, Moon Cups, tampons and yucky things like hot flushes.

One episode I had two weeks ago was when I was having a meeting with a 52 year-old cartoon is there in Dar es Salaam. He asked me what the menopause was. He had two grown up children, but perhaps not a grown up partner. So it was left to me to be the one to inform him, for his own good naturally. It went something like this:

"What is your subject content?"

"The Menopause"

"What is that?"

"Well, you know I sent you a text asking if you were already here?" (We were to meet at a coffee shop in an open square. It is absolutely boiling there, even without the menopause).

"Yes"

"Well, the reason I wanted to make sure that you were here before me, is that it is very hot here, and so I didn't want to wait for you. The reason I didn't want to have to wait for you, is because I get hot flushes as a result of the menopause. The menopause is like puberty".

I PAUSED IN CASE HE DIDN'T KNOW WHAT THAT WAS, HE NODDED.

"It is when your body changes as you get older and your periods stop. It takes 10 years just like puberty does".

"Oh I see, interesting, I didn't know. Is it all women"?

"Yes all women, British as well as Tanzanian"

"OK"

Moving swiftly on, he asked,

"What style of cartoon do you want for this? What is it called again?'

"MEN O PAUSE", I enunciate

He explained what he needed from me, which was some styles of cartoon I liked, along with an example of the text I had written.

We chatted a short while about the up coming election here and then parted. I sent him all the material he wanted within an hour.

I never heard from him again.

Do you think it was something I said?

A Singing Uterus Explains Menopause? YES

You must watch this. It is brilliant. Commissioned by Ellen Dolgen. I am trying to get visuals onto my blog but learning how to include a working you tube link is on the plan for next week. In the meantime, I am sure you can find it yourselves...

LINK TO: A Singing Uterus Explains Perimenopause and Menopause by Ellen Dolgen:

youtube.com/watch?v=W4TMJ7xyeaE

One Leg Better Than Two

No I haven't got George Orwell's Animal Farm wrong. I am in fact referring to massage. Like sport, it is very good to have massages. Helps with the "Exercise or Die" motto I have. It moves your darling blood around your veins and arteries and sorts out blockages.

As the body changes in the peri-menopausal period. Note the use of the word changes not ages. Both are correct, but I prefer changes myself. Whatever the word, I creak and groan and am very stiff. Fit but stiff. I go for weekly massages.

This self-inflicted pain is tremendous.

The masseuse of choice is called Fang. She always starts with my left leg, so as I am wincing with an elbow stuck into knotty sore bits, I lie there knowing that I have one more leg to go.

I have invented a new verb – to be Fang-ed. It is now in current use in my household. Whether I have been Fang-ed or am going to be Fang-ed at the weekend. This particular masseuse is the strongest I have ever met. I don't speak Thai, she doesn't speak English and so our limited conversations are in Kiswahili. Her English comprises – "relak Madame". I say, "I am trying," or now I say "I can't relak it hurts". She thinks I am a complete and utter pussy. Once she brought her colleague in, to explain to me that I had to be braver, and then it would all be fine.

I thought I had been brave.

I am always glad I have been through it all, when it is over though and I do feel much better. I especially like the pillow marks on my cheeks, where my face has been crushed. The other good look is the matted eyelashes. Not seen that? Try being face down or side on into a pillow for an hour, with mascara-ed eyelashes. Note the effect on arising. Instead of looking like you have hundreds of eye lashes. Is it hundreds? I look like I have 4. 1 blob on the top eyelid, all stuck together with mascara and the same at the bottom.

It is a good thing that with your body "changing" so does your vanity. Fuck it. What is wrong with doing the shopping afterwards with 4 eyelashes and lined, pillow prints on your face?

A Bit Tired?

Gosh my other list is 50 symptoms. This is only 35. I am now going to use this list. I know that I am breaking my head in the sand rule, BUT this might make someone out there feel better, when you can barely get through the day.

I recommend plenty of nod offs, power naps, lie downs, whatever you want to call them. A good time is when you have dropped children at school. Call work with bad hair or something like that and just lie down.

I had to lie down most of Thursday just to get over being such a busy bunny on Tuesday and Wednesday. I had to deal with an infestation of bees and snakes, evacuate the house for 24 hours and get married. Too much in one-week for a nice gal.

LINK TO: 35 symptoms of perimenopause adrenal fatigue:

theperimenopauseblog.com/35-symptoms-of-perimenopause-adrenal-fatigue-2

Read This – We Are Snookered

I was surprised and then not surprised by these findings from the Nuffield Health Menopause Survey:

nuffieldhealth.com/hospitals/news/menopause-symptoms-support

I've never used a link before I am not sure if it will work or not.

I am still tussling with technology.

How's Your Menopause Going Love?

Asks my darling 88 year-old father each time we speak. I bet he never spoke as much about the menopause with my mother, as he does with me. He knows about all the symptoms in grisly detail. He is a bit forgetful as he is elderly and I am a bit forgetful as I am menopausal, so I can repeat my stories merrily and he loves them each time.

He is Australian and still has an accent. "Struth love", he said last night when I told him my headaches were back. We reviewed my medication; he is always horrified how much I am on, as am I when I list them all out. He is also not that impressed with the bloody doctors.

I think I got my swearing gene from him. Australians, certainly my father, use bloody and don't think it is a swear word. Other words in my repertoire from him are, it is gone to buggery i.e. broken and stop fiddle arsing around with that – i.e. Get your mitts off my things. We all now still use it, as do all the grandchildren. He also calls us all Flight Sergeant, as other parents might say love or darling. He tried to sign up to fight in WW2, but they found out he was only 13, so he had to be satisfied with the Reserve Air Corps. This experience gave him a lot of new vocabulary, which stood him in good stead for later days.

My mother on the other hand really couldn't swear properly. We – her children – had to teach her all the proper words when we were teenagers. She liked the word wanker, but didn't always use it in the correct context so she wasn't allowed to use it when we were out. Talk about birdbrain this morning. It is all my darling little synaptic connections. I have an image of my mother going up the high street doing her shopping. Those were the days with the shopping trolley on wheels; they came in sensible colours and occasionally a suggestive tartan.

One day she was out and was flanked by two punk rockers. The male had a Mohawk and all the dog collars etc. reminiscent of the era. He was also pulling the trolley. The girl had a shaven head with a hint of pink still visible. A woman was also following all of them. When my mother stopped to go into a shop and left her trolley and the two punks outside, this woman scuttled over to her and asked her if she was all right and did she need the police. Were those punks threatening her? My mother laughed and thanked her, and told her they were her daughter and her daughter's boyfriend and they were helping her with the shopping.

Menopause Needs To Be Dragged Into The 21st Century

These two doctors are fab. They were part of the Nuffield Research. I love their outrage; it shows it comes from the heart.

Dr Julie Ayres, Specialist in Menopause and PMS at Nuffield Health Leeds, said:

"The issue needs to be dragged into the 21st century. Increasingly employers are beginning to take employee health and wellbeing seriously, with numerous initiatives to help improve health and fitness, yet clearly the menopause remains taboo. Until we shine a spotlight on the subject and try to tackle some of the difficulties that women are facing at work, we stand to lose experienced and talented women who should be at the peak of their career rather than facing forced retirement or feeling alienated.

I have many patients who couldn't cope with work without hormone replacement therapy and wouldn't even contemplate stopping until they retire. Any woman struggling in the workplace should seek help and look at all of the options available

Dr Annie Evans said:

"Increasingly the evidence shows appropriate hormone replacement therapy (HRT) to be suitable for many women, with far less risks than previously thought. The options should be carefully explained to each individual woman, in light of her own risks, future goals and the quality of life she is experiencing. It is an absolute tragedy that large numbers of women are getting no help at all."

The research suggests that despite the sheer numbers of women dealing with symptoms of hormone change and menopause, the subject remains taboo in the workplace. A staggering nine out of ten (90%) said they felt unable to talk to a manager or colleague at work. However, almost one in five (18%) said they have needed to take time off work and one in fifty (2%) of working age women with symptoms are on long-term sick leave.

The survey also flags up a number of barriers that menopause experts say may be causing thousands of women to miss out on advice, management strategies or treatment, which could significantly improve their quality of life.

Despite reporting symptoms like joint and muscle ache, hot flushes, irregular periods, night sweats, mood swings and poor memory, 45% of women questioned failed to recognise they could be experiencing symptoms linked to the menopause, with just under half (42%) mistakenly believing they are too young or too old for symptoms. A quarter simply put it down to stress.

Just over a third (38%) of women sought help from a GP. However, a quarter of those who visited a GP said the possibility of the symptoms being menopause related failed to come up.

This Week's Knowledge

OK for today we have boobs, heart, and pelvic floor i.e. front and back bottom, and depression. And then enough for the day. I am going to the gym. File, read, delete or just go to the gym.

In her ground breaking book, <u>The Female Brain</u>, physician and neurobiologist, Dr. Louann Brizendine, tackles the issue of hormones and depression in women. Intrigued by research data, which shows that women suffer from depression at a ratio of 2 to 1 compared to men.

It's Pelvic Floor Time – Squeeze, Two, Three

I couldn't do boobs without the pelvic floor now could I? I do super clenches during my gym classes. Remember to clench as you carry out your day to day activities and super clench at the gym. Then you will never need SAM, as you will never have LBLs.

The Pelvic Floor: Know the facts – take control Nuffield Health:

nuffieldhealth.com/blog/category/physiotherapy/pelvic-floor-know-facts-take-control

And Now For The Boob Piece

But remember when you are in the darling menopause phase, you are more likely to get heart disease. Shame about the small boobs not avoiding cancer, thought I would sneak in there...

LINK TO: Nuffield Health – Dispelling the Myths around Breast Cancer:

nuffieldhealth.com/blog/category/general/dispelling-myths-around-breast-cancer

And The Final Whammy

All right gals, we're doing the heart – last one for today. Pay close attention and read the small print before you reach for the chocolate. Then join the gym. I told you all you need to know is EXERCISE OR DIE. V easy really.

LINK TO: Nuffield Health – Women's Heart Disease and Cardiovascular Health:

nuffieldhealth.com/woman/heart-disease-cardiovascular

Oh No I Forgot Cholesterol

Whether it is your boobs, or your heart or other darling body parts. All the solutions are the same...EXERCISE OR DIE... So much easier than reading these articles when you have to look up each word.

LINK TO: Nuffield Health – The importance of tracking your cholesterol:

nuffieldhealth.com/blog/category/fitness-and-health/importance-tracking-your-cholesterol-0

I'm Not 34 Or 74

I'm 54 and you see the thing is that I don't look like these lovely young things in this picture. Neither do I look like the old ladies in the menopause pictures. The article is about heart disease and menopause but you would never guess from the photo. Maybe we could have some pics of gorgeous middle-aged women? Happy to pose but I do need notice to get my highlights topped up. They have slid down my head again.

Man Paws And Periods

We are avid Downton Abbey fans. I have bought Season 5 on i tunes and the latest episode downloads all day Monday so we can watch it in 3 chunks on Monday, Tuesday and Wednesday evenings. Actually we don't usually get to Wednesdays, it is so gripping.

In one of the episodes, Robert, Earl of Grantham, had been particularly cantankerous. My daughter piped up, "Maybe he has man paws. He is like dad was last weekend".

She knows that men don't get the menopause, well I think she does. I didn't understand all the hormonal details of the menopause, as it came and bit me on the bottom, who knows what a 9 year old can understand?

For example, the other day we were at the supermarket and a woman was having a complete strop. My little girl whispered to me," does she have the menopause mum?" It was then, I realised that in fact, she thought IT was visible and known to complete strangers.

We have talked about each and every woman we know well and less well. She has asked me about each and every one of them to know if they are having their "many paws" or not.

I thought she was fairly well informed about the mechanics of periods. There was no packet of tampons safe from her hands when she was young. She used to open them up and wear them as earrings to dress up AND share them with her then, other 4-year old friends. If there weren't enough milk bottles around for them all the feed their babies, a tampon was handy. I explained to her that I had to bring them from the UK. She would reply, "yes mama" and then forget next time they needed a pretendy feeding bottle. I had to hide them.

Once, I didn't hear her come into the bathroom and I got such a fright when she suddenly said boo, that my tampon nearly shot up to my chest. She always asked if she could pull the string out for me...

So she knew about eggs every month, not being used and coming out on a tampon. For years she knew this.

Last month she was going on her first overnight school trip. The school decided that they needed to have a talk with all the girls, in case any of them got their periods while they were away from home for this 24-hour stint. I was glad I knew in advance so I could tell her.

You just never can tell though can you? When I told her that her teacher was going to talk to her about periods she was surprised. "I thought they were going to talk about what clothes we had to bring", was her first reaction. "Why do we need to talk about periods"? When I explained it was in case, any of the girls GOT a period when they were away, she looked confused.

"But that won't be happening to me. I am only 9. It won't happen till I am old".

Neurotic or Highly Strung – Which Would You Prefer

I prefer highly-strung. What do you think? My friend said, "no you're a nutter and neurotic, it is different to being highly strung". We are both menopausal and as we were having a nice sit down, neither one of us could be bothered to get up to find a dictionary or something electronic to check on definitions.

Hmm now I have had a chance to look them up, I am not sure I am that impressed with either of them.

Taken from The Oxford English Dictionary. I tried other dictionaries for a definition, which, I thought, was better but there wasn't one.

Neurotic (In non-technical use) abnormally sensitive, obsessive, or anxious: he seemed a neurotic, self-obsessed character

Highly Strung Very nervous and easily upset highly strung horses

Well I know I am not a horse.
Soooooo, I think my friend may have a point. I didn't bother to look up nutter, as I know she meant that as a complement. I might check with her later today though...

Parking Between The Lines

Why is it so hard? I have spent years being able to practice the form of parking called abandonment. You stop wherever you want and turn off the engine. This technique was perfected in Namibia, where there are 1,000,000 people in the landmass of Europe.

Dar es Salaam was perfect nine years ago for this technique as well – hardly any cars, no car parks just wasteland to dump your car in.

Things change though, we now have tarmac car parks, all TOO small for the big fuck off 4 wheel drive cars we all have here. In THOSE days you did need those 4 wheelers. NOW the car parks are too small for them.

And too small for me.

For menopausal me, it has become a power struggle as I am always told off for parking incorrectly. Always by someone usually about 30 years my junior and who doesn't drive. Guards.

I feel sorry for these chaps, BUT I note that they don't tell men off, only me.

Others don't get told to park straight, only me.

Last week, was a bad week. I was that cartoon which has a nice smiley lady watering the garden, saying, gym, no alcohol, gardening and I still want to smack someone.

Plus – the guards stand right behind you to "help" you get out. I have spent nearly 30 years getting out of car parks all on my own. I swear someone will be injured if they do that again while chatting to their friends and not even looking for the other cars. Ahh. My blood pressure is boiling as I write. I need Xanax.

The other day, I got asked again to park straight in an empty car park. I got out and put up my hand and said no, no, no I am menopausal and I have been driving for 37 years, I will be 5 minutes so no.

He didn't know what I was saying as he speaks Maa. I wish I spoke Maa. I wonder what the word for menopausal is in Maa.

That reminds me, of a major meltdown in August. I was trying to park in my hub's car park. Yes, he has his own car park. No he doesn't. This car park is too small for all the cars. Anyway I was trying to fucking park my mahoosive old Toyota land cruiser in a space for a mini. There were about 4 guards supposedly helping me. Well they weren't. I was sweating and swearing. The air con was of course not working. I flipped, as you do, when you are peri-menopausal and you do that freaky, scary, losing it thing. I left the car blocking everything. I got out. I ignored them all. I went up to my hubs office. I got him out of a meeting. I sobbed and sniffled and asked him to park the car.

He did. What a hero. He didn't swear or sweat. He assessed the situation correctly, and didn't say anything to me; otherwise it might have been meltdown to the power of 10. Ever seen one? Scary fucking Mary.

I think he tipped the guards after I had gone.

Outraged Again From Tanzania

Yes I am outraged again.

I am a bit pissed off in fact.

One of my darling dogs woke me up at 4am to go for a pee. Her not me.

My darling daughter kept slinging her arm and leg over

me in the night – wallop, and keeping me awake.

So yes that adds up to me being rather DANGEROUS and UNBALANCED.

You know what is on my mind? It is those bloody photos.

You know the ones that went with the article on heart disease and menopause. But the photos were of 20 year olds. I realised that there is nothing in the middle. No photos in the middle of women between 20s and 60s or 70s. Menopause doesn't only strike at those with gray hair you know. It lasts a decade some of us were quite bouncy and energetic before. 50 is the new 40 they say. So WHERE ARE THE PHOTOS?

I think I may well have a parking problem later.

A Letter To My Body

Darling Body,

I love you so much.

You have been so good to me all these years.

I just wish I had done more human biology at school and since then, so that I had been better prepared for "our glorious decade".

I am so sorry that I had no fucking clue.

I am so sorry that doctors aren't trained properly to help us.

I am so sorry that we have been on 4 different types of HRT and based on that last note from the doctor, I don't think we have maxed out yet.

I am so sorry for the darling little parasites we have had nestled in our intestines this week and last.

I am so sorry for the meds, which are like barbed wire scraping around our guts to get rid of the little fuckers.

I am so sorry that I have been so rude to people and still want to tell everyone off most of the time.

Well I am not always that sorry, mostly it was their own fault, except very sorry to our darling daughter.

I am so sorry that there are no wonderful photos of us, in all that horrid research about us getting older, when we are quite gorgeous when our highlights are done.

Speaking of which I am so sorry when we have our armpits waxed. It hurts me more than you.

Your beloved and faithful friend

Out Of The Mouths Of Babes

The synaptic connection for this, is -thoughts I've been having since I wrote "Man Paws and Periods".

I remembered I wanted to tell you about over-hearing this conversation between my 9 year old and her 15-year-old cousin last summer. I do seem to spend an inordinate amount of time skulking and eavesdropping.

"Does your mum have the menopause?" My daughter asked.

"What's that?' he replied.

"When your mum gets grumpy and takes lots of tablets", she said importantly. She was rightly proud of her knowledge in comparison to the15 year old.

"Oh yes, I think mum told me something about that," he muttered. "She gets in bad moods".

"Does your mum take tablets?" My daughter persisted.

"I'm not sure, what for?" He replied.

"They help with mood swings", she sounded like a textbook.

"What are they?" He sounded lost.

Well when your mum shouts at you, especially at bedtime.

I Can't Stop Twitching

I just did something IMPROMPTU.

I just went outside to collect a parcel from a friend and saw my next-door neighbour. It was fate, I was supposed to talk to him about cutting down the diseased trees on our shared wall, but I had been putting it off.

I strode over, what a sweetie he is. I went in and walked round his garden. Beautiful banana, lime and orange trees. He and his also elderly wife love gardening.

My life has been so highly scheduled for the 33 years I have been working, that I rarely do anything impromptu like that.

I was starting to feel twitchy when I was walking around.

While I was chatting to him, I was simultaneously talking to myself and saying,

I am doing something that is not on today's list

I am doing something that is not on today's list

I am doing something that is not on today's list

OMG Do I have time to do something that is not on today's list

OMG Do I have time to do something that is not on today's list

I don't have my watch on, and I don't have my phone.

I don't have my watch on, and I don't have my phone.

I came inside for Xanax, I was twitching, as I was SO OFF LIST.

Years of working for large organisations, in conflict areas, in jobs which are not, in fact, as such, humanly do-able, but that everyone does anyway, with an average 60% of staff needed at any one time – fucks you up. No, I did not breath during that sentence.

Then I started running my own business, which closed in June after three years. Considering that and my glorious decade, it has all rendered me rather unhinged. Or neurotic or highly-strung. Definitely unhinged this week and last. Definitely.

Plus it causes twitching in impromptu, off list situations.

No wonder the fanny doctor says steady ship for a year. Only 4 months in.

I know why I am unhinged this week particularly and last come to think of it. I started a course Screw Work Let's Play. Utterly Brilliant. Do it if you can.

BUT I realised that I am not really coping with all the juggling of my various projects and bloody life, which gets in the way. I am half Scottish and am really into dance and folk music. Wherever I have lived in the world, I've always been part of the Caledonian Society and usually on the demonstration dance team.

I recall a St Andrews Ball in Colombo, Sri Lanka in 1984,where there was a sudden curfew called because of unrest. We all HAD to stay till 6am when it was lifted. Fantastic. A friend just reminded me of her doing a sword dance at 4am for the whole assembly. Even though it was many years ago, it still seems to haunt her. My recollection was that she was brilliant, and didn't trip at all. No one would have known anyway.

Anyway back to Tanzania and the present.

November is the busiest month in the Scottish Season here and I run the junior Scottish Dancing group with a friend. We have 3 performances next week. I also run a drama club, as I feel it is important that children understand recent history starting withWW1, and then celebrate the anniversary of the signing of the Convention on The Rights of The Child.

So drama last week. Another show tomorrow.

Why is it ALL the same month?

I started time logging all my projects and I LOVE IT. I JUST LOVE IT.

But my body has been freaking out, and my brain is telling me,

OVERLOAD, OVERLOAD

I know that I am really completely rubbish at stopping and breathing.

You can tell I have only taken two breaths the whole time I have been typing.

Coming Out Part Two

"Why have you got Ruby's baby rag and why are you sweating so much?" asked her little friend.
"I've got the menopause and I am very hot". I replied.

"What's that?"

"Well the body is a wonderful machine..." I start off

You like so far readers?

"Just like your body is changing as you get older, taller and stronger, bodies change all the time, as you get older. For example when you are waiting for a baby...and when you get older then, your body keeps on changing and that is called the menopause, just like puberty".

"Ahh I see"

"Can I have something else to eat?"

Well even a month ago, who would have thought it?

I shouted to a 9 year old. It's so great, children aren't shifty at all, they just listen and then move on.

I'm keen to hone my message and delivery as I usually have 30 seconds.

Any thoughts or feedback? I thought it was quite good even though I say it myself.

Weddings and Amoebas

Actually last week was rather full on, so that might have added to my stress levels.

I found vermin on Monday

I got Rentokil in on Tuesday and couldn't stay in the house because the poison was so strong.

I had to evacuate self, child, hubs and 6 animals for a group sleepover at a friend's.

I got married on Wednesday morning. We are legal in Scotland but not in England. I am a HUMANIST...

I got amoebic dysentery on Thursday

Hubs woke up with huge puffy eyes on Thursday

We don't think getting married causes them.

My Daily Dose

The spell check drives me CRAZY, though it is often hilarious with what it comes up with.

For example I needed to type the names of the drug I am taking for my amoebas. It is Diloxanide Furoate. You would not believed the number of times I had to tussle with the bloody machine to get in what I wanted rather than what the computer wanted.

First it came out as Diloxanide FRUIT

And then Diloxanide FUR OATS

When I keyed in dysentery just now, it came out as SYSTEM TRAY.

Heat Seeking Missiles

"It must be love, love, love... it must be love, love, love..."
The Specials song is so wonderful.

We have a huge family bed. However I have noticed that
no matter how big the bed, I can't escape them. Either of
them, they just want to hug. My daughter throws her legs
and arms all over me, so does my hubs. It is terrible when
I am trapped in the middle, sweating away. I gently move
them over, but after 5 minutes they are fucking back. We
end up in a tiny huddle in about a quarter of the bed. I
know I should be grateful for the love, but often I just
want them to STAY IN THEIR SPOT and let me have
the air con on.

What a horrendous night last night.

All right here goes. My hubs is away, so daughter is in our
bed from her bedtime. She always comes in during the
night anyway. It took us more time than usual to put the
net down. It has a new tear in it, courtesy of THAT LEG
when he got into bed one night last week and got tangled
in the net.

We were both asleep, but my daughter has a cold, so she
wanted the air con off. I was sweltering and on the edge
of the huge bed as usual – in my place.

So I left and went into her bed. All to myself and air con

on full. Bliss.

Until I got found. She hopped in and the air con went off.

I woke up at 2am absolutely sweltering and trapped between daughter and the wall. She had the whole bed I thought. I then looked up and heard snoring. A dog was next to her with her head on the pillow. There was also a dog on the bed at our feet.

They aren't allowed on the bed.

"It must be love, love, love..."

Shall I Show You How To Use The Printer?

Those words made me break out into a sweat at 09.24 this morning. I am in my flow, writing and having lots of fabulous thorts.

Hubs is back from a trip, and his first thing for the day, having slept in, is to get my new phone and re-booted computer back up onto the home printer.

This is where we celebrate difference. I am unable to multi-task anymore, because of being in my glorious decade, but he is.

He thinks, "I see the printer has been stuck for 7 days

while I was away, I will be thortful and change the settings on her computer, yes, I will just go and ask her to bring me her computer now and she can stand there and watch me to see how to do it..."

I think, "please don't make me give you my computer when I am in the middle of writing something, so you can sort out the settings..."

While I WATCH you

In a room with no air con and a broken fan

While you give me instructions

I will not be able to listen to or remember because I can't focus, not because I am trying to hurt your feelings..."

Catch Me If You Can

It's 6.30am here in lovely Masaki. That's 3.30am in rather chillier UK. It was 32 degrees here by 6am.

It's Wednesday. Only Wednesday I should say. This week I have dropped my child for the school bus three times.

Yes, you say, so have millions of other adults done that around the world.

Yes, but on two of those days this week, I forgot my child.

I took the dogs, but not her.

The dogs were amazing; they started barking as soon as I took off, this morning. I wondered what was wrong and then realised. I turned round and was back in the drive before she came out.

I drive the car out of the compound while she is doing her last minute sun cream and mossie repellent. I wait outside the gate for her. Or not, as the case maybe.
The reason for my distraction? Well I am so, so excited. I have had a great idea for a menopause app. I am doing this wonderful course and one of the items on offer was personality profiling. Well, I call it that; the clever man who invented it calls it a great name – Wealth Dynamics. That's very posh. He has worked out, that there are 8 personality types contributing to the wealth of themselves, their families, their community etc. Guess what I am a Creator/Dynamo. I never would have guessed in a million years I was creative. I always thought that was drawing, painting, elegant dancing in contortion like positions, and writing deep, dark tomes with a message.

Well having ideas is creative. WOW.

So now I have permission, to live in my bubble of self-centredness when I am excited and so full of ideas I can't get them written down quick enough.

Except no, the clever report I got, showed me how I need to manage those attributes, which go with this creator type personality, so I don't leave the rest of my world behind, and feel resentful when my child is hungry at 5pm.

A new friend said a clever thing recently that the impact of menopause mood swings were personality dependent. If you are a really patient and lovely woman already, then your mood swing might be more like a less lovely woman on a good day. Makes sense really.

Give me a week to calm down a bit and I hope to have worked it all out...or not...that's the thing with ideas, you never can tell about their execution until you give them a go. Another tutorial on offer was how to design an app. I thought that was for software people, then I read the blurb and an idea just popped in. Just like that.

In the meantime I took a Xanax just now, as I was a bit hyper and need to calm down, otherwise my brain gets to overload. I also need to try and think of others.

My child doesn't know that I left her behind on either Monday or Wednesday. My hubs know though that I fell asleep last night at 7pm with my child. Fatal that lie down for a quick cuddle... hmmm. I haven't actually, as such, seen him yet this morning.

I feel a spot of light grovelling coming on.

Onwards and upwards.

2.30am Again

I did NOT mean to fall asleep at 9pm with my daughter.
How many times have I said that?
My daughter had woken up boiling hot and put the air
con on. It was2.30am and I was in my spot squashed
between her and the wall. Eileen was in her spot at the
bottom of my daughter's bed. Strange, my hubs usually
puts the girls out when he gets in. He must be getting soft
in his old age.

Rebecca was in her spot on the rug. She can get from
there to under the bed in a nano second, when she hears
hub's car arriving. Her tail sticks out from under the bed,
but she thinks he can't see her, because she can't see him.

I get up and check the time. Daughter has gone back to
sleep.

"Where shall I go now," I muttered to myself. It is really
hot, I need air con. It doesn't work very well in the living
room but I headed for there anyway.

I got my work from my bedroom, the dogs on my heels, and started working.

Suddenly the dogs are both on the sofa, pretending to be asleep.

"Off Eileen, off Rebecca, "I say sternly.

They completely ignore me. They are so disobedient.

They love me so much, but they don't obey me

I tell them to get down again, they look in shock, that I have said it twice. I mean it this time and I push and poke them off. They play dead and refuse to move themselves.

They last about 2 minutes on the floor, plotting and waiting for me to get engrossed in something. Then when I was busy Rebecca sidled onto one sofa, so stealthily I don't notice, or that is what she thought. All part of the plan you see. Then Eileen saw her sister doing it, so she waited 10 minutes and then she did the same. She oozed her way on, like a snake. First one paw, then another and then she flattened her tummy and wriggled on and then one back paw and then the last paw. Triumph and she quickly closed her eyes to look pretendy asleep.

I glare at Rebecca, she plays cute, looking just too unbearably sweet for words, wags her tail, huge brown eyes looking at me limpidly.

I glare at Eileen, whose tactics are completely different from her sister's. She looks at me reproachfully, as if to say, "what? I was asleep you know."

We go through the whole routine again.

After the third go. I have had enough and give up.

"Don't think I don't know you aren't on," I shouted at them whisperingly. You know how you do when you don't want to wake the other mammals in the house. Rebecca wags her tail ready to be cute and Eileen shuts her eyes tighter and pretends to snore.

The sofa gets so hairy, I know it is horrible. My hubs has come a long way in his relationship with dogs, from natural enemy to being spotted patting them and blowing kisses. But he has a limit with beds and sofas.

"What are those dogs doing on the sofa," he bellowed, giving us all a fright. Rebecca and Eileen were off the bloody sofas in a trice, and stood to attention. He opened the door and off they trotted.

"Just put them out," he said. Just like that. "Just put them out."

"But they scratch at the window when they see me, in here and they are a pest."

"Who is in charge?" he asked.

"They are", I replied, especially at 2.30am.

Deodorant In My Hair

It was bound to happen. For over a year I have been meaning to move either the deodorant or the hairspray from the same shelf. It was an accident waiting to happen, I kept saying to myself, and then forgetting 2 seconds later.

It was either going to be hairspray in my armpits or deodorant in my hair.

Yesterday it was the latter. The hair spray has NOW been moved.

Ditto

Well I am not sure what else to say except maybe it wasn't 2.30am, maybe it was 3.00am. But the dogs and me were the same i.e. I was awake when I shouldn't have been.

The part that was different was hub's guest appearance. At 4.30am the living room door crashed open. He walked into the living room and straight OUT of it through the front door to the garden. 4 pairs of eyes followed him. I could tell that the dogs were thinking the same as me, "where IS he going?'

He came back inside after a few minutes and proceeded to do the same in reverse. I asked him what he was doing. "Turning water pumps on", he muttered and returned to bed.

Never a dull moment in my life in the early hours.

"Peri", some of you may know, is a Latin prefix meaning..."

Some wonderful quotes I found this week

"I'm what is known as perimenopausal. "Peri", some of you may know, is a Latin prefix meaning 'SHUT YOUR FLIPPIN' PIE HOLE". So says Celia Rivenbark.

"Estrogen deficient women are the walking dead." — Marie Hoag MBA. I am with Marie on that. When I was estrogen deficient I was also the working dead.

Stefano Hatfield is editor-in-chief of High50. He turned 50 and feisty recently. Love the lumping bit. Haven't I been saying the very same thing?

"Society will be begin to shift its perspective. There will be more 50+ intern schemes, more back to work initiatives for over-50s. The image libraries may stop lumping 51 and 75-year-olds together as silver surfers, and we may all get our heads around the notion that we have to provide for our parents and even our grandparents' care.

The elastic generation knows it has to deal with all of this and the brutal reality that our dependent children will have no money for years to come and no longer empty the nest. But, we will cope with it all and more. Fitter and more energetic than any previous 50+ generation in history, we cannot and will not be bent out of shape..."

Hurrah for Stefano.

Getting to the Heart of the Matter

You know that I keep myself up to date with menopause pieces, in order that you don't have to. Even though I scare myself to bits sometimes. Here are the goodies from the last two weeks:

Getting to the Heart of the Matter: Recognize the Symptoms of a Heart Attack – the No. 1 Killer of Women By Ellen Dolgen. It is worth reading this article of Ellen's again and keeping aspirin with you at all times.

I also read that Mariella Frostrup was in difficulty with her medical insurance company deciding that her menopause treatment couldn't be covered as the menopause is classified as natural. I had fun classifying this piece. Men and Menopause, Menopause in the 21st Century. Menopause Awareness. All those and more show how UNaware people and institutions are to menopausal women. Fortunately Mariella wasn't going to take this sitting down and fought back with this great line;

I listened to Women's Hour on Radio 4 last week. The subject was the menopause and frankly, I felt sorry for all women after it. The female specialist doctors were arguing with each other in that hilarious British way:

"Well I am sorry Valerie (or something like that), (SHE ISNT REALLY SORRY AT ALL) but you will find that the evidence is not with you on that point..."

"Well Hilary (or something like that), I think you will find that that is not quite right. (COMPLETELY BLOODY WRONG) and that there is evidence to prove that synthetic HRT made from paper is better than..."

When asked about how it is possible to take a detailed history in the time allocated for an appointment in the UK:

"Oh of course I can take a woman's detailed history in a nano second..." (I AM FANTASTIC)

"Well I can take a woman's detailed history in probably

less than a nano second without even asking any questions.." (I AM MORE FANTASTIC)

There was a male hormone specialist being interviewed. I am not trying to look for problems just because he was a man, but he had such a monotone voice and sounded SO bored. The pace was frantic and my friend and I who were listening in – felt even more confused at the end. It is really not helpful when the doctors are arguing amongst themselves.

To be fair they were trying to cram too much into one session and it is good that they aired the subject at all. In British speak that means it was really CRAP and that they should have done MILES better in researching for the show in the first place.

Attacked By A Strapless Bra

Maybe it is just me. Is it just me? Does anyone else have a violent strapless bra?

I wore it with my swanky dress to the St Andrew's Ball two weeks ago. It started slowly chaffing as the air con failed to keep up with the rising heat from the dancing bodies. After a while I thought I was going to self combust and NEED stitches as the wire was poking through into my sternum.

I went into the bathroom and took it off.

Oh the relief.

I had another bad clothing episode recently as well. Last Saturday there was a yoga workshop for menopausal women. Well there was some confusion as to what the women were clearly in other women's minds as there age range was huge. Anyway having had to stand in the middle of the circle, I was really feeling fairly "outed". Worse was to come though, I had worn nylon track suit bottoms and a drip – fit nylon top. These are what I wear for yoga as the gym I go to has air conditioning. This place didn't have air conditioning and it was absolutely boiling. I thought I was going to pass out it was so hot. Yes, well you can imagine.

I ended up doing the second glorious hour of yoga in my bra and (big) pants.

Laura Ashley Dresses

Imagine me in a big flouncy Laura Ashley dress – the early 90s. I didn't know that for years people thought I was a modern nun. When someone told me, I replied, "but I wore lipstick". "Yes," they said, "a modern nun with a big dress and lipstick".

I worked in the Caribbean from 1990 – 1994 and one of

the activities I was doing was fundraising for children who were disabled. There are lots of rich people who own islands and I was after them.

There was one tourist island I went to- the name will come to me in a moment – the social worker and I were the only 2 people dressed. Everyone else was either naked, semi naked or in the owner's case wearing shorts and his teeth. I had my best Laura Ashley on and my colleague from the Ministry of Social Welfare was neck to knee in frilly, pink taffeta. The owner was this rich American, whose father had bought the island in the days when you were allowed to do such things.

He was very pleasant, but he had such ill fitting dentures it was hard to concentrate on my pitch.

The long and the short of it was that he wasn't going to support services for disabled children, he preferred to fund the footballs and the football league. When I pointed out that that was for boys not children and so thought perhaps he could add something specific for girls, his teeth nearly fell out.

I can't remember why that came to me and why I wanted to share it. Must be Christmas coming up and all that. Goodwill to all humankind and all that.

I Want My Afternoons Back

I need my energy for the afternoons.

If I take a happy tab, I'm sleepy and a bit dopey.

If I don't, then I am horrid.

What to do?

I want the afternoons back.

They left with my hormones.

I have high hopes they will all return in 2015.

Kiddy Paws

"If you and dad get to have temper tantrums because of the "many paws", then I get to have them as well. Mine will be called "Kiddy Paws.""

What Exactly Is High Blood Pressure?

You don't know either. I was trying to bluster an answer to my 9 year old when she asked what a blood pressure machine was for. I realised I didn't know.

I have looked it up for you on the Blood Pressure UK site;

"If you have high blood pressure, this higher pressure puts extra strain on your heart and blood vessels. Over time, this extra strain increases your risk of a heart attack or stroke. High blood pressure can also cause heart and kidney disease, and is closely linked to some forms of dementia".

Usual solutions exercise, don't drink and eat too much.

They are always the same.

December Bloods

I am off to Dracula's office tomorrow for my December blood tests.

I am very excited, I hope my hormones and other bits and bobs are progressing in the right direction.

The Latest Intel...

I love the abbreviation of the word intelligence. I heard it on Spooks, a spy drama programme, which I love. I have adopted it into my current vocabulary. Not sure if it should have two ll's?

I think it would be fair to say that I was in a bit of a fog earlier on in the year. Despite having a new great doctor, I have still been unclear what tablets I am on and why. I feel rather shifty admitting it, but I might as well. It might make someone else feel better in case they are the same as me. I finally got round to asking the doctor what each of the HRT tablets and patches were for. I also asked her about progesterone.

"The supplements that you are receiving are two types of oestrogen; the transdermal medications (gel and patches) are oestradiol and the tablets deliver oestrogen via the gut wall and liver and convert to a different type of oestrogen called oestrone. In the peri-menopause and early post-menopause, it is important to have the mix of both types of oestrogen which work in a synergistic way. The patches and tablets give a slow delivery into the circulation albeit in a low dose and the gel is very much a short acting boost should you need it but probably would not be much more use than this as the half-life is only 4-6 hours. Most women either use it first thing in the morning or to reduce the afternoon slump which I think was your difficult time.

At some stage, we will need to add in a progesterone to provide endometrial protection. It is important not to do that until your low oestrogen symptoms are resolved"

You may remember that she had asked me about sugar and carbohydrates and that I had to cut sugar and the carbohydrates out. I was confused as I had done, so I made an appointment with the menopause nutritionist. Isn't that fantastic, that they even have one.

I went through the issues that the doctor had first raised with me in July. It seems like an eternity ago now.

The one I hadn't fully understood is this insulin resistance piece. It is on the diabetes continuum. Can be controlled so it doesn't get worse but needs even more radical diet changes than I had realised. This, with the HRT could be the secret to me getting my afternoons back from the fire-breathing monster who inhabits my afternoon body at the moment.

Managing The Holidays

It is time I managed my holidays like a grown up. I read Ellen Dolgen's blog – it is great – and was stunned she had a piece on managing holidays. Gosh I thought, she has been here before.

"Hair Today, Gone Tomorrow" Ho, Ho, Ho

Ellen has done a really good piece on can why your head hair starts to shed and why it lands on your chin instead. I am still checking for chin hair but it hasn't arrived yet.

I do suffer regularly from head lice, courtesy from having a child at primary school. The other night I went to a ladies Christmas dinner thing. It was lovely, but I had a terrible cold and a temperature, so wasn't on my best form. Included in the price was either a mini-manicure, mini-pedicure or a mini-foot massage. Or so I thought. It turns out the message I got was wrong. It was a head massage, not a foot massage.

I duly went ahead with the head massage, even though I don't really like them. My friend sensibly said, "just change and have a foot one instead", but there was a queue and as usual I didn't think.

I shouldn't have submitted. It was horrid and I didn't enjoy it one bit. Everybody else who chose to have a head massage loved them. BUT NOT ME. NO WAY

The shoulder bit was ok, but I prefer to grimace in private, not when I am scrubbed up in my posh frock. Then when the masseuse moved up to massage my head, my hair came out in HANDFULS.

Plus it was SO itchy, I realised that the bloody head lice eggs were starting to twitch and were just loving all this attention.

Unlike me.

Menopause Wanabees... Oh Yes

Who would have believed it in August when I got back from holiday? Here I was in November, at a friend's 40th birthday lunch, holding court over the other 10 women aged 30 something...ish.

There was one other woman my age. We were both having hot flushes. I told the group, that as I had organised it, we were inside with aircon, and I hoped that was ok with them all, given my condition and all that. "And mine", she chipped in. A fellow hot flush sufferer, I asked her, "which year are you in of your glorious decade?"

She replied, "year 3, you?"

I announced "year 3 as well". We gave each other a high 5. I then got out my pill purse and tipped it out on the table. Everyone gasped and then cheered. I gave my new friend one of my quick acting get sachets as she was having a bit of a moment. She clearly didn't generally out herself quite as much as I did, but was loving it. The Laurent and Perrier champagne also helped. Her, not me, I don't drink alcohol, as I am too sensitive – as you all know.

My god asked the others, how do you remember, which to take when?

I then proceeded to show them my systems of bleeps, clicks, harps sounds and doorbell buzzes, which get me through each day.

But the best was when I said, "it's awful, but you do have that liberating thought on a regular basis, which is I'm menopausal, I'm over 50 and fuck it, I can do what I want and I don't have to worry about what other people think any more..." "Amen to that," said my new friend. "yes, fuck it, if I have to put up with hot flushes, and forgetting everything, then I don't need to put up with other shit any more..."

Someone said, "I want that now, I aspire to be menopausal if I get that...

What a great moment. Being me is COOL.

About The Author

Deborah Crowe is an ex-teacher and aid worker of 30 years, currently living in Dar es Salaam, Tanzania. Friends and family used to laugh at her descriptions of her fraught peri-menopausal days. She uses humour to create awareness of the need for women to take better care of themselves so that they can help save the planet.

DOGS IN DAR

A lady dog's insight into how her owner's deal with stress - or not - as the case may be. This will make you wonder if Eileen has a point. "Humans should learn from us, we don't need chocolate and tablets to get to sleep..."

This cartoon comic strip is set in Dar es Salaam, Tanzania, where the author lives. Deborah Crowe has written several stories based on her dogs' views on humans. Humans like herself who don't sleep enough, work too much and are too stressed. There will be more comic strips to come.

WWW.DEBORAHJCROWE.COM **TO GET DOGS IN DAR FREE THE DARLING MENOPAUSE - THE SHOCK**
A humourous diary about the discovery of the peri-menopausal world and life lessons from it.

"How long do you think it will last?" I asked. Thinking about two weeks with a course of antibiotics.☒"Oh about ten years," he replied merrily. "No", I screamed, "No. No. No. I need to sleep sometime in the next ten years...I didn't really do that of course. I was too conditioned for that.

Come and find out what I DID do.

WWW.DEBORAHJCROWE.COM **TO GET THE DARLING MENOPAUSE - THE SHOCK**
REVIEWS

Wonderful writing, full of wry humour and a light-hearted look at life as we struggle to maintain our composure and keep a brave face during turbulent times. I thoroughly enjoyed reading it and could identify with the author's experiences. A great read to reassure yourself that you are not alone – cheered me up no end!

THE DARLING MENOPAUSE - SORTED

Diary part two - coming out the other end of the peri menopause - with yet more life lessons. It is not just the hormones.

"I THINK THE HRT you have been taking COULD CAUSE YOU TO HAVE A STROKE AND SO YOU NEED TO COME OFF THEM NOW - TODAY - IMMEDIATELY..." I realised that had I had it ALL WRONG. It wasn't the hormones fault, it was the lifestyle for too many years - too much work, too much stress and not enough down time. My body just came and bit me on the bum to make me pay attention until I learnt how to redress the balance."

WWW.DEBORAHJCROWE.COM **TO GET THE DARLING MENOPAUSE - SORTED OUT IN MARCH 2017**

21784658R00085

Printed in Great Britain
by Amazon